INSIGHTS: GOD'S USE OF EARTHLY INHABITANTS FOR HIS KINGDOM PURPOSES

With *Special Insights* Into the Work of a Servant-Prophet

by
Prophetess Mary L. Johnson-Gordon

Copyright © 2011 by Prophetess Mary L. Johnson-Gordon

Insights: God's Use of Earthly Inhabitants
For His Kingdom Purposes
With Special Insights Into the Work of a Servant-Prophet
by Prophetess Mary L. Johnson-Gordon

Printed in the United States of America

ISBN 9781613794500

All rights reserved solely by the author. The author guarantees all contents are original and do not infringe upon the legal rights of any other person or work. No part of this book may be reproduced in any form without the permission of the author. The views expressed in this book are not necessarily those of the publisher.

Unless otherwise indicated, Bible quotations are taken from *The New King James Version* of the *Bible.* Copyright © 1996 by Thomas Nelson, Inc.

Copyediting
Royalene Doyle
Doyle Writing Services
doylewrites@comcast.net

www.xulonpress.com

A Message to the Readers of This Book............... vii
**From the Desk of Prophetess
Mary L. Johnson-Gordon**

**Introduction: The Lord's Clarion
Call Remains**... xi
   Unto Eternal Life: Be Obedient in
   Your Response.. xiii
   The Unexpected, Awe-Inspiring Path of
   Progress—God's Way...................................... xxvi
   Observations of Other Fully Human
   Servants at Work... xxxi

**On The Job Training: Serving, Learning
and Teaching,** 37
   In Italy.. 39
   In The Nations of Israel and Cambodia............... 44
   In Congo, Africa... 57

The Presence of God in China 75
   Prophet on Assignment..................................... 77
   Angelic Assistance 82

v

Insights: God's Use Of Earthly Inhabitants...

Observe: The Prophet's Journey, Process to
Victory and the Lord's Horsemen
Sent Into Battle..85

Occupy Until His Return **103**
The Work of the Servant-Prophet Can
Be Very Stressful...105
Tamper With the Traditions of Man for
Me! Says the Lord..108

For Your Consideration............................... **115**

A Message to the Readers of This Book
From the Desk of Prophetess Mary L. Johnson-Gordon

Oh what an honor and privilege it is to be an earthly vessel considered worthy of the Lord's service—serving the Kingdom purposes of God! My delights and pleasures have prompted me to share my experiences with the hope of providing **insights** into the ways of God in this first book of the INSIGHTS series.

This book is purposed to open the windows of *revelation* for you, and show the true, active and dynamic ways God works <u>through</u> His people on this earth—to accomplish His Kingdom purposes <u>with</u> heaven's prospective in mind. From these examples of my personal journey with the Lord in ministry, and **my** interaction with other Servants of the Lord, I hope to encourage you in your own Spiritual/Servant endeavors and build your expectations of what the Lord may yet ask of you.

Insights: God's Use Of Earthly Inhabitants...

As for me, in my station in life, I am serving in the Office of Prophet, where much writing is required. Therefore, I am often referred to as a Scribal Prophet. This Office has required much *personal time* with the Lord! It has also increased my need for International travels, and my assignments have become more and more intense—both nationally and internationally. Over the past ten years I have gone on more than 40 individual foreign mission trips to different Countries and to an untold number of Nations within these various transcontinental journeys. Many have required repeated visits to the same nations. Continental Africa has been my most widely traveled.

For *Insights* into the nations work, I have chosen to share a few of my experiences in various nations: Italy, Israel, Cambodia, China, and Africa. These include overcoming significant hardships—by God's divine intervention—experienced in Congo, Africa. However difficult these times have been, the Lord has never left me! Wherever the Lord sends me I must go, with the assurance that He is my Companion, my Keeper and my Sustaining Source.

In the process of walking in obedience to The Lord's Call and Station in life for me, I have witnessed countless miracles; and, at the Lord's bidding I have also received and delivered numerous and strategically important—yet difficult—prophetic messages. To assure me of my *called place of service* He has

viii

repeatedly sent me to Psalms 96 in His Scriptures. Then He would say, *"You are called to the nations. Ascribe your heart and go forth. I will teach you in the field of your going."* Often, He would simply say, *"Come walk on the waters with me."*

No one, single event, has been more powerful or more significant than another. **All have been and are required for such a time as this!** I am reminded by the words of Elihu (the young friend of Job), *"If they obey and serve Him, they shall spend their days in prosperity...but if they do not obey, they shall perish...and they shall die without knowledge"* (Job 36:11-12). It is not God's desire that any should perish and be forever separated from His Presence. Therefore, it is imperative that we set our hearts on the *heart-desires* of Jesus, Himself, which He revealed when speaking to Nicodemus: *"...so must the Son of Man be lifted up, that whoever believes in Him should not perish but have eternal life"* (John 3:14).

Perhaps, **you** are called to step up into the front-lines for the cause of Christ! If so, *Go Forth.* Walk in Obedience; and *Be NOT Afraid* for the Lord your God will have prepared the way for you! Have no doubt! As your heart beats with excitement and perhaps a bit of apprehension, while reading this book, be assured that both The Lord and His Host of Heaven— including *Heaven's Inhabitants*—will be at your disposal. So then, yield your will, and go forth, while

Insights: God's Use Of Earthly Inhabitants...

purposing in your heart to fulfill His ***destiny place of purposes*** for your tomorrows.

IN Jesus name!
May God Greatly Bless ALL who have ears to hear...

Prophetess Mary L. Johnson-Gordon

INTRODUCTION

The Lord's Clarion Call Remains

Unto Eternal Life
Be Obedient In Your Response and
I Will Make You Fishers of Men

Dear Reader, you must know that the writing of this book is about you and the privilege that the Lord, Himself, presents to you. In these End Times—these Strategic Times in History—He has impressed upon my heart-of-understanding that I am to emphasize the need for workers. *Workers are sorely needed,* He said. It starts with your obedience to the Will of God, and ends with a victorious <u>finished</u> work!

God uses yielded earthly inhabitants, ordinary people on this earth, for His Kingdom Purposes today—even as He has done throughout all of history—including the time and Person of Our Lord and Savior Jesus Christ. However, I must stress that there is a readiness process for all servants. It

> My purpose is to share, teach and speak directly to you from the mouth of these printed pages—into your Hearts of Potentiality!

starts with our sold out obedience to the will of God. Then, with acceptance of the *servant-hood processes,* and perseverance through every hardship, there is rendered a Victorious, Finished Work!

Where will workers be found? From the lowliness of *dirt,* Earth-man was created. God breathed the breath of life into his nostrils and he became a living creature who fell short of his potential. But because of the work of Christ, fallen man—*Earth-man*—can be formed into valuable, usable instruments for God's Kingdom Purposes today. That's you, and that's me, whom He must equip for our uniquely individual missions.

The work of the Lord God is being done not only by *Earth-man Dwellers*—that is *Earthly Inhabitants*—but also through the transcendence and transmigration of *God-man Dwellers*—the *Heavenly Inhabitants*—who work between the dimensions of heaven and earth. This is vitally necessary and strategic to the Plans of God for mankind. Essential to the urgent End Time work of God, He has deemed it necessary for a more collaborative, cohesive, co-existent, and co-laboring process. This process encompasses Heaven's and Earth's Inhabitants working in harmony, transcending and transmigrating—moving between dimensions—in order to meet specific, strategic needs!

Even as I complete this book, the Lord is leading me (requiring of me) to produce a series of insightful publications/writings. Soon, two more books will be published which are designed to give further insights into other dimensions of service—more *Insights* into the Transcendence of Visitations for the Cause of Christ. The next books will provide greater Insights into Fourth Dimension work. Working titles/concepts include: <u>Sights and Activities Witnessed in Heaven With Special Insights Into God's Use of His Heavenly Inhabitants on Earth</u>, and <u>The Cause-Driven Life: A Re-call to Church Leaders for the Rendering of More Effective Services for His Kingdom Purposes</u>. The Lord does not want His people to *perish for lack of knowledge.* So it is that He will use His *Earthly Inhabitant Prophets* to speak and write His insightful messages—to motivate others to accept His Clarion Call.

I say to you, there is immeasurable potential within you for God's Kingdom purposes!

It is essentially imperative however, that any discussion of Servant-hood—**Authentic** Servant-hood—be established and discussed by the example set forth in the Life and Person of our LORD and Savior Jesus Christ over 2000 years ago. **He led by example. And He became the Finisher of His work!** As we allow Him to be our model in the *processes* of readiness and the *execution* of our assignments on earth, we too will be *finishers* of our course for His Kingdom Purposes. Our victory is assured and secured—by Him!

Insights: God's Use Of Earthly Inhabitants...

Yes! Victory is guaranteed! He is the *Guarantee* through the *Full Measure* of Who He IS: Jesus Christ, the Risen Savior and Son of God; Second Person in the Godhead; working in harmony with the Person of the Holy Spirit and the Host of Heaven. These include the residing Eternal Dwellers/Heavenly Inhabitants who are at His command! The *Full Measure* of His limitless Authority, Power and Heavenly assistance is ours to be experienced, as His Authentic Servants. We must emulate His *attributes* and *character qualities* by His Grace toward us.

An essential part of the work of our Ministry Assignments is the continuous engagement in Prayer-communications with Heaven. The Bible tells us that: The *Prayers of the righteous avail much.* There is Power in Prayer! But, when the Lord spoke to me of these things, for the purposes of application to a nation's work, He emphasized and enhanced His words saying: ***Prayer Creates—Prayer Changes— it can Create an <u>Atmospheric Womb</u> for birthing the Will of God on earth!***

By example, Jesus was and is a Prayer Warrior; a Miracle Worker and Healer of the sick; Contender for Justice, Liberty and true Freedom. Wherever He went to serve, Signs and Wonders followed! He contended with man's religious errors and evil spirits found in men-on-earth. In short, He did *exploits*! He was endowed with Power to do so! Then, as Jesus prepared for His Eternal, <u>Finished Work</u>, He said: *"Most assuredly, I say to you, he who believes in Me,*

xvi

the works that I do he will do also; and greater works than these he will do..." (John 14:12, NKJV).

We are expected to do no less! We should <u>expect</u> to see visions, and then be able to pray according to God's will with Signs, Wonders and Manifestation of change prevailing! **There is power in expectancy!**

Be clear, however, and know that we (you and I) must continually *yield* to the processes of being <u>Called</u>, <u>Equipped</u> and then <u>Sent</u>. Let us also be clear about the fact that even Jesus became weak and weary. Heaven responded to His need by sending two of *Heaven's Inhabitants/Eternity Dwellers*—Moses and Elijah—to comfort and encourage Him on the Mount of Transfiguration. Jesus was strengthened and enabled to fulfill His ultimate *Destiny-Place* in the Will of God—on the Cross—for <u>us</u>! We, too, must <u>claim</u> one ultimate, undeniable fact: The *dependability* of God IS SURE! On this Foundation alone is all Faith, Trust and Hope built and sustained. In this working process, <u>Divine protection is our privilege</u>, and with the Host of Heaven—including *Heaven's Inhabitants*—at our disposal, we can be assured that Victory is ours!

We must also understand that *family brokenness* is <u>no excuse</u> to retreat from the Call. God loves and uses broken people and He made this crystal clear in the lineage of Jesus—being fully Son of God, fully human/son of man (see Matthew 1: 1-17 and Luke 3: 23-38). Jesus' roots traced in biblical genealogy

Insights: God's Use Of Earthly Inhabitants...

show Him in direct association with many broken people. He inherited the human legacy of pain—His *family* experienced pain. Exploring just a few of the very early biblical records we find family members with deep character flaws and serious problems: **Adam** was cast out of an ideal situation because of disobedience (Genesis 3:24). **Seth** was a baby conceived out of the grief caused by one brother's murder and another's alienation—actually named as a *substitute child* by his heartbroken mother (Genesis 4:25). **Noah** brings us to the Bible's first case of alcohol abuse. Noah caused an embarrassment to his sons during a drunken stupor in which he laid naked (Genesis 9:20-23). The family lineage of Jesus continued to expose multiple family *dysfunctions* throughout all the centuries, even to the time of Jesus' conception, when the dark cloud of suspicion and accusation surrounded Mary and Joseph.

However, Jesus did not allow His broken *family history* to distract, discourage or detain Him! **He accepted Himself as the Son of God, and purposed to walk in obedience toward His *Destiny-Place*; He walked in His Calling—to the Finish!** He became the solution, not only for His earthly family's brokenness and pain, but to the world's continuing generations of brokenness—providing the Way to Eternal wholeness.

This, Too, Is Our Good and True Example To Follow!

Jesus, the **_fully human man_**, was born to the virgin Mary and as such, was subject to the Laws of Moses concerning, for example, the requirement for circumcision. He had to be circumcised, just as all other Jewish males. The apostle Luke spoke to this truth in his teachings:

> *"And when eight days were completed for the circumcision of the Child, His name was called Jesus ... [and] when the days of her [Mary's] purification according to the law of Moses were completed, they brought Him [Jesus] to Jerusalem to present Him to the Lord..."* (Luke 2:21-22).

Then, Mary received a prophetic word from Simeon, a just and devout man who lived in Jerusalem, and who was led by the Holy Spirit to go to the Temple <u>that day</u>. When Simeon came upon

Insights: God's Use Of Earthly Inhabitants...

Joseph, Mary and Jesus he blessed them, then spoke directly to Mary saying:

*"Behold, this Child is **destined** for the fall and rising of many in Israel, and for a **sign** which will be spoken against (yes, a sword will pierce through your own soul also), that the thoughts of many hearts may be revealed"* (Luke 2:33-35).

"...They returned to Galilee, to their own city, Nazareth. And the Child grew and became strong in spirit, filled with wisdom; and the grace of God was upon Him" (Luke 2:39-40).

Twelve years later, the Family returned to Jerusalem—returned to The Temple to celebrate the Passover Festival. Luke's writings allow us to witness Jesus' *Bar Mitzvah* preparations (possibly His actual Bar Mitzvah). Jesus demonstrated that He had been weaned from his Mother's teachings, had experienced years of instruction by His earthly father, and was now accepting his new role—His *Bar Mitzvah* role as *Son-of-the Covenant*. And His WISDOM far exceeded anything the priests had seen before! *"And all who heard Him were astonished at His understanding and answers."* (Luke 2:47). Jesus had BECOME a ***scholar*** at the young age of 12 years old! To reflect accurately on Jesus' scholarship is to understand that WE TOO must become scholars— the educating part of the process of our *equipping*!

xx

Insights: God's Use Of Earthly Inhabitants...

In His fully human state, Jesus came to understand that He was destined for *Great Works* in His special relationship to/with His Heavenly Father. Yet, being young and eager to begin His journey, He remained behind—exercising His best *young* judgment—without His parent's knowledge or consent. They were, with cause, concerned for Him. When they found Him, He asked His anxious parents, *"Why did you seek Me? Did you not know that I must be about My Father's business?"* (Luke 2:49).

Luke's writings continue, telling us that *Jesus increased in wisdom and stature, and in favor with God and men* (Luke 2:52). He had to complete His process of maturation. We, too, will make immature mistakes. But the good news is that we are also given grace and the favor of God as we experience our shortcomings and learn from them.

Also, like Jesus, we must <u>complete</u> our process of maturation and training. Later in His life, before Jesus began His Ministry in earnest, John the Baptist baptized Jesus in the waters of the River Jordan. There, Jesus had an encounter with the Holy Spirit of God:

When all the people were baptized, it came to pass that Jesus also was baptized; and while He prayed, the heaven was opened. And the Holy Spirit descended in bodily form like a dove upon Him, and a voice came from heaven which said, "You are My beloved Son; in You I am well pleased." Luke 3:21-22

Insights: God's Use Of Earthly Inhabitants...

God, the Father, was confirming Their Father-and-Son relationship and expressing His pleasure with Jesus' growth and preparation for service! In this baptism experience, Jesus had been baptized with water <u>and</u> in the Holy Spirit. NOW He was <u>equipped</u> with Power to do greater works and to withstand Satan's temptations. But, it was also a *testing time.*

In my experience I have learned NOT to expect to be able to do any good works for the Lord without the enabling Power of the Holy Spirit! *Testing Times* will come—for certain! You Must BE Equipped not only to withstand temptation, but to <u>Execute Good Works</u> according to the Will of God! The Triune Godhead experience and relationship is foundational for any dimension of useable service in His Kingdom work of purposes.

In Acts 1:8 we hear Jesus speak these words:
"But, you shall have Power when the Holy Spirit comes upon you; and you shall be witnesses to Me in Jerusalem, and in all Judea and Samaria, ***and to the end of the earth."***

The path of readiness for Jesus' works was <u>in Process and in Progress</u>. Observe the ***process*** as He overcomes the devil, written about in Luke 4:1-13.

Then Jesus, being filled with the Holy Spirit, returned from the Jordan and was led by the Spirit into the wilderness, being tempted for forty days by the devil. And in those days He ate nothing, and afterward, when they had ended, He was hungry. And the devil said to Him, "If You are the Son of God, command this stone to become bread."

But Jesus answered him, saying, "It is written, 'Man shall not live by bread alone, but by every word of God.'"

Then the devil, taking Him up on a high mountain, showed Him all the kingdoms of the world in a moment of time. And the devil said to Him, "All this authority I will give You, and their glory; for this has been delivered to me, and I give it to whomever I wish. Therefore, if You will worship before me, all will be Yours."

And Jesus answered and said to him, "Get behind Me, Satan! For it is written, 'You shall worship the Lord your God, and Him only you shall serve.'"

Then he brought Him to Jerusalem, set Him on the pinnacle of the temple, and said to Him, "If You are the Son of God, throw Yourself down from here. For it is written: 'He shall give His angels charge over you, To keep you,' and, 'In their hands they shall bear you up, Lest you dash your foot against a stone.'"

Insights: God's Use Of Earthly Inhabitants...

And Jesus answered and said to him, "It has been said, 'You shall not tempt the Lord your God.'"

Now when the devil had ended every temptation, he departed from Him until an opportune time.

Jesus clearly and specifically remembered and spoke the WORD of God to counter the devil's deceptive attacks! Yet the devil "departed" only to prepare new schemes.

Please know that Satan will return again—at a more *opportune* time—at the times when you are the weakest! So, watch and pray! Eat the Words of God. Surround yourself with Spirit-filled brothers and sisters in Christ, and remain strong!

In Reflection: Jesus knew the Word and He was equipped by the Holy Spirit who would guide Him accurately in His answers to the devil. It was vital that Jesus was already prepared to withstand the test. Now, He could be assisted by the Holy Spirit in all His times of testing!

We, too—the Present Day Earthly Inhabitants who God will use for His Kingdom Purposes—must be *equipped* and *full* of the Holy Spirit before our testing time! We must follow the process of readiness for the uncertain hours of confrontation with the enemy wherever he decides to confront us!

Insights: God's Use Of Earthly Inhabitants...

In Observation: Jesus **overcame** by quoting the written Words of God in response to each of Satan's temptations. But Satan decided to use the same written Words of God in his attempt to confuse Jesus. Satan also knows the Word of God—often better than we do.

The Unexpected, Awe-Inspiring Path of Progress—God's Way

After withstanding the tests of Satan...

> *Then Jesus returned in the power of the Spirit to Galilee, and news of Him went out through all the surrounding region. And He taught in their synagogues, being glorified by all* (Luke 4:14-15).

However, in Nazareth where He had been brought up, He was rejected! Think it not strange when you, too, are rejected in your own city or community! A Prophet is seldom honored among his own family!

> *So He came to Nazareth, where He had been brought up. And as His custom was, He went into the synagogue on the Sabbath day, and stood up to read. And He was handed the book of the prophet Isaiah. And when He had opened the book, He found the place where it was written:*

Insights: God's Use Of Earthly Inhabitants...

The Spirit of the Lord is upon Me,
Because He has anointed Me to preach the gospel
to the poor;
He has sent Me to heal the brokenhearted,
To proclaim liberty to the captives and recovery
of sight to the blind,
To set at liberty those who are oppressed;
To proclaim the acceptable year of the Lord.
(Luke 4: 16-19)

My Dear Friends, be sure of this: <u>You are called to do no less than that which Jesus spoke and proclaimed in this passage of Scripture!</u> He was actually proclaiming, declaring and announcing His *Own* Presence among them—the Anointed One—Their Messiah!

They were all amazed as He continued saying:

"You will surely say this proverb to Me, 'Physician, heal yourself! Whatever we have heard done in Capernaum, do also here in Your country.'" Then He said, "Assuredly, I say to you, <u>no prophet is accepted in his own country.</u> But I tell you truly, many widows were in Israel in the days of Elijah, when the heaven was shut up three years and six months, and there was a great famine throughout all the land; but to none of them was Elijah sent except to Zarephath, in the region of Sidon, to a woman who was a widow (Luke 4:23-26).

AGAIN, in reflection and insight, I ask you, Dear Reader: To whom are you sent? To the great multi-

xxvii

Insights: God's Use Of Earthly Inhabitants...

tudes? To the lepers? Or to the one person who has the attention of God's heart?

Observe: Jesus also commented (see Luke 4:27-30) that there were many lepers in Israel in the time of Elijah the Prophet, and <u>none</u> of them were cleansed, <u>except Naaman the Syrian</u>. This incited much wrath among the synagogue teachers who were listening to Him that day. Jesus had to escape for His Life!

This *example* of Jesus' ministry shows us that we might not be able to accomplish all we desire in one location. Yet, we must move on and persevere! Jesus went to Capernaum where He cast out demons, taught with authority, rebuked unclean spirits forbidding them to speak—revealing Himself as the Christ—and commanded the unclean spirits to "Come Out!" And, the reports went out across the Region! (see Luke 31-37).

I EMPLORE YOU! Never become discouraged and quit! BE like Jesus and purpose in your heart to do "even greater works," every time you face adversity—just as Jesus did!

Jesus healed Simon's Mother-in-law. She had a high fever, and what did Jesus do? He stood over her, rebuked the fever, and it left her! She immediately rose and served them—Jesus and his disciples—the *friends* her son-in-law had brought to their home. The results which Jesus purposed in His heart are exemplified here also! (see Luke 4:38-39).

Insights: God's Use Of Earthly Inhabitants...

He traveled by day and *healed* the sick by night. He laid His hands upon everyone, healing them of various diseases, casting out demons...then departed to a "deserted place." Crowds were now following Him and they tried to keep Him from leaving. *"...But, He said to them: 'I must preach the Kingdom of God to the other cities also, because for this purpose I have been sent"* (Luke 4:40-43).

WE, TOO, must stay focused and go to the places we are sent—<u>without distraction</u>—just as Jesus did! Jesus left the synagogues of the cities and went to the *desert place!* He put the needs of the broken-hearted before His own conveniences and the cheering of His admirers. Those people *adored* Him after He healed them. This would have been a source of temptation for many servants. But, Jesus had been tempted by greater offerings in the wilderness. So now, this experience was pale in comparison to the rewards—the blessing of touching even more people with the Kingdom message—in other cities and throughout the Region.

Jesus stayed FOCUSED on His ***God-Sent-Purposes*** in spite of man's persuasions and appeals! So must we! He had already been tempted by environmental/ desert hardships and *mountain experiences.* So they were of no effect upon Him! From His adversities He gained strength. <u>There is strength in adversity, IF we persevere</u>!

Might we benefit by examining ourselves to determine if *we* are accepting *environmental tempta-*

tions? Are we too comfortable in our air-conditioned churches and homes, and refusing to GO where our *SENT-Purpose* leads—a place out of our comfort zone? God forbid!

Are we spending too much time and resources on *Mountain Retreats* as opportunities *get away* and *forget?* Are we running away from problems instead of using Jesus' examples and <u>applying the Power and Authority</u>, afforded to us on the Cross, to address our needs? Have Retreats and Mountain-top experiences become places of *idolatry* and a shrine of vain religion to escape disorder in the home (unpaid bills; unkempt, unsupervised children; unresolved relationships)? God forbid!

If Jesus had accepted His temptation(s), it would have forfeited His Authority Position—His Honor and Command-ability—and, yes, His personal relationship with His Father! It would have cost Him TOO MUCH! This remembrance must remain before us as we reflect on Jesus as our Example. Let us not forfeit our Authority-position by accepting temptation! We have the Power to make the choice NOT to accept it!

Jesus simply commanded Satan—speaking just a few specific and commanding words—saying: *GET BEHIND ME, SATAN!* (Luke 4:8). He discounted the significance of Satan's words! He took **authority over them** by His own spoken words which were <u>greater</u>! WE MUST REMEMBER HIS EXAMPLE, and take authority over every diabolical scheme of the enemy!

Observations of Other *Fully Human* Servants At Work
Co-laborers in God's Causes

Let us now reflect briefly on some other notable *Fully Human Servants* who followed Jesus' example and <u>purposed in their hearts</u> to "Be used of God" and they did great and mighty works.

The Prophet Isaiah is such an example. This particular story begins in 2 Chronicles 26. It was a season of great prosperity with National greatness under King Uzziah who enjoyed fifty-two years of godly leadership. Yet the Nation was about to undergo judgment, after King Uzziah's death.

The Lord revealed this secret truth to Isaiah (Isaiah 6:8-10), and asked: *"Whom shall I send* [to warn them], *who will go **for Us**?"* Isaiah replied: *"Here am I! Send me."* And so God sent Isaiah to Judah, knowing that most of the people would reject His message.

Insights: God's Use Of Earthly Inhabitants...

Was this some trick? No, it was not! Are these the Ways of God, as you know about Him? Maybe not! Yet, in this case, Isaiah was in dialogue with God about the true conditions of the Nation. And the Lord asked: *"Whom shall WE send...FOR...US?"* Isaiah did not hesitate to offer up himself as the sacrificial offering to GO! He found in himself a solution to God's revealed need, without apparent consideration for the degree of risk associated with his choice to be the one sent! Isaiah's ***cause*** and ***function*** (his responsibility) was to DELIVER the Word. That was his obligation as God's Servant!

Perhaps there will be times in your life as well, when you will be challenged to step out of your comfort zone into the sacrificial place of service. I trust you will recall and be benefited by these teachings. Remember, Isaiah <u>was sent</u> on what might seem like a futile assignment—as most people did not accept the Message. However, that was not his place to worry about. His *place* was to fulfill a revealed need—for Kingdom Purposes!

Furthermore, Isaiah the Prophet's decision—to offer himself as a *willing vessel*—provided an opportunity for a Nation to ESCAPE the judgment! (Isaiah 6:10). The king was a godly man, but the people were persistently rebellious! They brought the judgment upon themselves by their disobedience! The penalties of moral and spiritual decline resulted in the consequences of judgment. He chose to serve anyway even though this was not his issue to resolve.

Insights: God's Use Of Earthly Inhabitants...

When we say "yes, send me," it often results in the disruption of our normal lifestyles and sometimes requires <u>a career change</u>. So, let's be clear. The service of a *Yielded Servant* does not come without <u>significant cost</u>. However, there are also **Eternal Rewards beyond our imagination!** As we reflect on the lives of other Servants, you will observe that each had a Personal Encounter with God; each accepted a job/career change(s); each completed A Special Task for A Special Need, purposed to fulfill their ministry assignment(s).

- Jesus was a carpenter. He left His carpentry career after hearing His Father's voice at the River Jordan (Matthew 3:17), and took up His Cross to bring Salvation to the world.
- Isaiah was a prophet. He was called to the Throne Room of Heaven in a vision where he encountered God (Isaiah 6: 1-9), and accepted the Lord's call to "be sent" to the nations.
- Moses was an abandoned child who was adopted into the privileged household of Pharaoh. He had a *Burning Bush* encounter with God and became the feet-on-the-ground leader/deliverer of a Nation of three million people. (Exodus 3:1-10)
- Gideon was a farmer who was met by an Angel and became the leader/deliverer of his Nation (Judges 6: 11-14).
- David was a boy shepherd, who by faith killed a giant and became a king (1Samuel 16:1-13).
- Esther was an orphan, raised by an Uncle in a tiny village. She became a Queen and saved the Jewish Nation from extinction (Book of Esther).

Insights: God's Use Of Earthly Inhabitants...

- Joseph was an outspoken "favorite" child, who angered his brothers to the point of hatred, and was sold as a slave. Then his career changes really multiplied (identified as *Market-Place Ministry Stations*), until he became second only in power to the Pharaoh—ALL for Kingdom Purposes! All directed by God for His Covenant/ Kingdom GOOD! (Genesis 37).
- Mary was an average teenager making plans to live a normal, married life. Then an Angel visited her and she accepted the Call and Purpose to be the Mother of Jesus (Matthew 1:18-25).
- And, Saul/Paul was an educated Pharisee and a Roman citizen who actively persecuted Christians. He had a Damascus Road encounter with God, was temporarily blinded, then made a major career change to become possibly the greatest of all missionaries (Acts 9:1-23).

GOD IS THE SAME TODAY, YESTERDAY and FOREVER!

An authentically *Called* Servant—Prophet of God—will have God-Encounters in the process of recognizing and fulfilling the divine purpose for ones existence upon this earth. He is not his own, but IS a *Servant* of God who takes his command and instructions from God and walks in obedience to fulfill every assignment with all diligence!

A *Servant-Prophet* is a Chosen One, an *Instrument* on earth, serving for the benefit of God's people. He *speaks*

xxxiv

Insights: God's Use Of Earthly Inhabitants...

God's Words. And again, I must say, he or she is <u>not</u> his or her own. He walks in God's Ways; Speaks God's revealed Truths. He is God's Agent, not man's ambassador who applies his own wisdom to earth's circumstances. The Prophet expresses Heaven's Words of Truth!

FINALLY, I am mandated to caution all those concerning their *fledgling about in the distant place.* The Lord calls it, *"The Yonder Place of existence, away from God."* (I understand this concept, especially after one knows that He has a work for you to do!) It is vitally important that WE STAY IN HIS PRESENCE!

The Lord says, *Tell them that:*

> ➤ *In My Presence is Sweetness, Peace and Life-Bearing Substance! Outside of My Presence there is NO Sweet Yonder! No Peace, or Plenty or Life Abundance! No 'yonder place' is of ME.*
> ➤ *Stay in MY Presence! There is plenty of sweetness and love! Yonder places of the mind have led many astray. Teach on 'yonder places' away from me!*
> ➤ *The 'Yonder Place' is identified as the places where <u>conference-hoppers</u> and <u>church-hoppers</u> attend without roots,* He said.

Then the LORD led me to these three quoted Scriptures:

Is this not the fast that I have chosen:
To loose the bonds of wickedness,
To undo the heavy burdens,

xxxv

Insights: God's Use Of Earthly Inhabitants...

To let the oppressed go free,
And that you break every yoke?
Is it not to share your bread with the hungry,
And that you bring to your house the poor who
are cast out;
When you see the naked, that you cover him,
And not hide yourself from your own flesh?
(Isaiah 58:6-7)

Then shall you delight yourself in the LORD; and
I will cause you to ride on the high hills of the
earth, and feed you with the heritage of Jacob,
your Father. The mouth of the LORD has spoken
(Isaiah 58:14).

And the Lord said: *If you diligently heed the voice*
of the Lord your God and do what is right in His
sight, give ear to His commandments and keep
all His statutes, I will put none of the diseases on
you which I have brought on the Egyptians. For
I am the Lord who heals you" (Exodus 15:26).

In short, we must BE DOERS of the Word! We must BE FINISHERS of the Work to which we are called. And, we should expect to **BE the ones who will do Great Exploits for the Kingdom of God**! By God's Grace, I am a Witness—a Living, Participating Witness—to the Works and Will of God on Earth and In Heaven! I have experienced God and the God-kind on numerous occasions. I now offer to you a few examples of my personal experience—Life and Legacy—as a Servant-Prophet in the Hands of God!

On-The-Job *Training*
SERVING, LEARNING
And TEACHING

In Italy

IN 2006, I traveled with an anointed Ministry Team to beautiful Italy. There I experienced a Living Witness Encounter with The Lord which has increased my understandings of the **Strategically Applied Ways and Works of God**. You see, IF yielded, the Lord will continue to *grow* us throughout all of our lives.

On one day of the mission, the Lord mandated that I would stay in my room for a portion of the day. In this secluded place of obedience, the Spirit of the Lord came upon me with penetrating lights to my brain, which increased in intensity to enormous proportions. Then, the Lord showed me many things, including dominant spirits of error, which are in operation in Italy and the region.

Two of the spirits outran others as they approached me, and they were competing for the *name* of MARY. They were saying: "I want to wear your name—wear your name." Their mouths were moving in animated movements of the lips! I could see no teeth, but I could

Insights: God's Use Of Earthly Inhabitants...

hear clearly their words saying, "I want to *wear* your name!" The spirit with the pale face gave her request before the spirit one of color.

"LORD, of what spirit is this?" I asked.

He responded by saying, *What is your name?*

"Mary," I said.

There is a Spirit-of-Mary over this land, He continued, *NOT of JESUS, but of Mary. It is error personified in a name, meaning well, but in error of My ways, and of Me, The Risen One! Have Compassion on them, that they might know the Truth.*

Then He continued with His teachings, saying: *Remember—you saw more than one Nation of <u>people</u>* [these were people/nation <u>spirits</u>]. *Some were Black. They had approached you with the same request! The mouths were of different race and nationality—different, but the request was the same: "Let me wear your name."*

They know that there is <u>power</u> in the name, but they don't know <u>which</u> Name. They can't distinguish between the names of Jesus and Mary. They believe them the same. Error! Error! Error!

The Lord continued, saying: *When they* **know better** *they will <u>do better</u>! See? Over and over you have heard the word TRUTH out of the mouths of your Tour Guides. They yearn for the* **knowing** *of Truth. They SEEK* *after it, but Truth has escaped their reality, perception and minds, beyond the <u>traditions</u> of worship. SEE?* said the LORD.

Mother Mary makes them quake—NOT JESUS—Who they know not of by experience. To Mary they bow down ritualistically.

Then the LORD spoke loudly! *TAMPER WITH THE TRADITIONS OF MAN FOR ME!*

Later that evening, at the Healing Services, I was troubled by that which had been revealed. I *prayed* and *prayed* for correction—defending the Cause of Christ: His Honor! Then I observed that the Evening Service's Songs of Praise were all about JESUS! The Ministry Team Leader's opening words, given before the Anointing and Healing service began, were all about that which **Jesus will do**! And with each Miracle thereafter, everything was about **that which Jesus did**, including the drama presentation which was all about the ***Power* of Jesus**. The *credits* were His! Jesus was on display! And He Blessed! His corrections were being made within this diverse multi-ethnic audience. Many miracles were performed!

<u>THE BODY OF WATERS</u>

Just as we finished our Italy Mission Tour, the Lord showed me a vision of a body of water, or brook, likened to one that might be seen in a park. It had large boulders lying about in different places. The water was crystal clear/clean and beautiful, and was about

Insights: God's Use Of Earthly Inhabitants...

waist deep—just deep enough to wade in, dip in, jump in, without harm to anyone. The Lord later referred to this area as a place of *A Tidal Baptism—A Refreshing of The Spirit!*

As I observed the open vision scene before me, I noticed that people began to come to this body of waters, all of them with joyful hearts. Then one by one they began to jump into the water with clothes on! They were *baptizing themselves!*

Noticeably, some of the children—who were great among the numbers—were jumping into the water sideways. But they were <u>not</u> playing! They were dipping and rising with great *joy*! They didn't seem to care that there were no Clergy present to assist them.

I thought, Lord God, they want Water Baptism by *emersion!* There is no one there to satisfy their desires for Baptism, so they are Baptizing themselves! And, they are feeling refreshed afterwards!

Praise God! He again reminded me of His words: **Tamper with the traditions of man for Me!** And so it is that I offer this Vision and Testimony to you, my Readers, for your *edification, and enlightenment*—for your prayerful considerations to join in the co-labor-ship of correcting error through

> I charge you even as I am charged: Tamper with the traditions (erroneous traditions) of man For the Cause Of Christ!

Insights: God's Use Of Earthly Inhabitants...

Gospel Truths—shining the Light of Christ in the dark places of the world.

In The Nations of Israel and Cambodia

The Lord released a *very special, unique and strategic anointing—apportioned* by His grace—to meet the needs of nations here, as special prophetic garments of color were required of the Prophet.

In February of 2007, I was again with a Missions Team, this time in Israel and Cambodia. Throughout the several weeks after my return home, the LORD continued to unfold revelation after revelation relative to His **Manifested Presence there.** I shall attempt to share my experiences, revelations and understandings as revealed to me—and for you, the Reader's instruction/illumination—while giving ALL the GLORY and HONOR to GOD! For I am only a servant...a mere *breath* of His nostrils.

This Account Is About God's Nation Works: His Revelation Insights into His WAYS

(A supernatural act is taking place at this moment of writing: Colors of deep **bluish purple**, **red** and **olive green** are manifesting, as bleeding through the words I am writing. I have no immediate understanding of the significance, except to understand that it is a God phenomenon. However, I do understand the color **red** to mean *discipleship* and it is also the color of Royalty in its duty to engage in war to defend land and people. **Olive green** indicates *prophecy*.)

During the Team's Morning Prayer and Praise Services, prayers were being sent up on behalf of Israel—I was speaking the heart of God for Israel—when suddenly, I felt the Spirit of God and could not stand. Then the LORD showed me His Presence in living, pulsating and moving colors of magnificent **BLUES**; yet it is difficult to describe the precise shades. The colors hovered over Israel, but more specifically over Bethlehem and over Jerusalem—in that order. Both cities resided on opposite sides of a wall. I believe the BLUE color represents Salvation, Peace, Faith and Rest.

(Again, the words are changing to **red** and **green** colors; even these words of note have taken on the color of **red**. For two days I attempted to write this, but each time the strangeness

Insights: God's Use Of Earthly Inhabitants...

of colors began again. There is no empirical knowledge or reasoning for these occurrences. They are happening supernaturally!)

The encounter of His Miraculous Presence (manifested in the color of BLUE) was indeed one of God's special Divine, Supernatural moments in time! It was also one of His Sovereign Moments to release His **Special Anointing.** He *hovered* there over Israel, in displays of indescribable beauty! But my mind quickly attended to the thoughts of *Blue Night Lights* and places where Blue Lights are used for caution and safety at night time.

As I looked at the scene, there was a double stratum of Blue Hues in Living Colors which seemed to be merging—adjusting and merging! These were not natural lights, but a far span of *color* across the horizons—one over and over the other. I understand this represented many things including His Love, His Peace, His Salvation and most importantly, His desire for this Nation—Bethlehem and Jerusalem— to UNITE as One People/Nation—UNDER GOD! (The use of the words **over...over**, as impressed upon my mind, is meant to impress upon your minds the *positional posture* of God's Love for ALL His People. Thus, the layer upon layer/over and over is interpreted.)

The LORD revealed that He had released from Heaven, a colorful, *Prophetic Anointing* to meet the needs of these factional People/Nation. As He revealed Himself—His Presence—to me in Living

Colors, He said that He had released an anointing that He called *An Indigo-Anointing*. Twice He repeated: *The Indigo Anointing is a Provision for a Nation—It is a Provision for a Nation! It is the color of Blue-Violet. It is for Love, Peace, Salvation and Rest from struggles and contention,* He explained.

Again, by His Sovereign Will, He saw fit to orchestrate and arrange for the use of Prophetic garments to be worn on the occasion of His choosing! This *act* was not unlike the Prophets of old when some were required to wear strange garments and do strange things to make a Prophetic Point— *Prophetic Garments for a Prophetic Moment!*

Then the LORD released A Prophetic *Act of Significance*.

While preparing for this trip, the LORD prompted me to take my two-piece *Blue and Gold* African garment, which was made for me while on a Mission to Nigeria, Africa eight years before. I was also to take my new Blue and White *Jewish Prayer Shawl*. In obedience, I did so. But, I wondered, at what point I would be afforded an opportunity to wear an African dress in Israel?

Then, I was reminded of the major miracles accomplished there in that Nation of Nigeria, Africa where the dress was made for me OVER NIGHT after the supernatural, miraculous healing of the natural

Insights: God's Use Of Earthly Inhabitants...

heart of the husband of the Princess. Thereafter, we won *favor* with the King, whereby we became his guest for dinner! While there, I was privileged to pray and *minister* to the King, under the power of an exceptionally heavy anointing! The Spirit of the Lord overshadowed him and he went into a trance-like state of sleep. As he came into consciousness, he began to give this testimony of his Spiritual encounter saying: "I have had prayer many times before. But, as this Lady began to pray, I went somewhere! I don't know where I went, but something happened to my heart! It seemed like my old heart was removed and I was given a new one!" He continued trying to have everyone present understand this supernatural encounter that he had just experienced! The reality is that his *Spiritual heart* was changed during his encounter with the Lord!! PRAISE GOD!

Consequently, a Nation was also changed because that King held a significant Governmental position of Finances. He received a Prophetic Word given me by the Lord on behalf of the suffering children of Africa, which was to be corrected from his position of strength in which God placed him, as King! He now had the *Position of Power* and the Equipping to do the will of God for the Children! He now had the opportunity to become a *Market-Place Minister*, you see! He heard and he received the word with expressions and testimony of his profound encounter with God that day! Then, he called his neighbors and all of his own children in for prayer and blessings!

Insights: God's Use Of Earthly Inhabitants...

This then (God's directions to wear *Prophetic Garments of Clothing* of specific colors and style), was and is about changes taking place in the Nation of Israel and, indeed, the World! We must see/understand that we are being used as *Change Agents* in the Nations. God uses Ministers and He uses Ministries in strange and unique ways to **change nations!**

(The colors are again *bleeding through*, within seconds of my writing a certain word.)

THE OPPORTUNITY ARRIVED for the wearing of the Prophetic Dress, on the night of the Saturday Sabbath, Jewish *Shabbat*, when disturbance erupted between the Jews and the Moslems. Prayers at the Wailing Wall were aborted, and our buses returned to the Hotel, where a proper Shabbat Dinner Feast was prepared, complete with the lighting of TWO candles—one going in and one leaving out.

This was to be the LORD's fine moment of opportunity to have His Will and His Way—to dress according to His plan and His good pleasure. I wore the African dress, watched and prayed for understanding. I was surely in the dark of my own understanding. But, The LORD soon began to reveal the Prophetic connections and significance, one garment-piece at a time (**look closely at the garments shown in the back cover photo**).

(At this point of writing, the colors are manifesting again.)

Insights: God's Use Of Earthly Inhabitants...

This TWO-PIECE, Blue and Gold dress was to be worn TOGETHER, to make ONE fine garment suitable to wear in the presence of THE KING. It was to be worn at one of God's *fine Prophetic Moments-in-Time*, not just at a dinner event.

Within a detailed description of this garment much significance was revealed. The TOP part of the dress—Electric Blue in color—was ornately decorated with Braids of Gold over the shoulders, and it had a straight, long companion skirt. When worn together, the dress *became* <u>one</u> Elegant Dress, indeed, *fit* to be worn in the presence of a KING. The Lord then revealed to me that, symbolically, the <u>top</u> of the outfit was likened to the elegance of the Golden Dome. But, when worn with its companion long skirt, it *became ONE* Elegant dress, fit to be worn in a KING'S Presence! Further He revealed that...

* ✳ The TWO PIECE dress represented the <u>factional parts</u> of a Nation:
* ✳ When joined properly together, the two parts become ONE Nation
* ✳ They will BECOME a FIT, WHOLE garment in the Hands of God
* ✳ A BRIDE-in-WAITING, dressed in His Salvation colors of BLUE
* ✳ Dressed and waiting for His Return!

The *provisions* were/are there—in place—for the *taking*. HE has PAID THE COST—for Peace and Hope—ON THE CROSS OF CALVARY.

Insights: God's Use Of Earthly Inhabitants...

Further revelation became clear as I understood that God was doing something with the concept of the number TWO position of the Godhead. It is/was evident in the patterns and numbers. JESUS is second in the Godhead position of Father, Son and Holy Spirit.

Now my attention was drawn to the SECOND garment that I was required to wear that evening—a *Jewish Prayer Shawl*. I wore the shawl over my left **shoulder** and over my heart. I attached it to my dress with a hand-carved broach of a **wooden dove**, which carried a **spray of olive branches** in its mouth.

I am reminded that God GAVE HOPE through the *wooden cross*, and He SENT to us the gift of the Holy Spirit—for Power—to effectuate change upon the Earth. So we should expect to operate in Power—HIS Power—to do His Will.

The LORD has previously said: *"The greatest need of the Jews is the acknowledgement that Jesus Christ is LORD."*

I felt a bit over-dressed, but now I was fully conscious of the *Prophetic Acts required and the need of wearing Specific Garments;* the Significant Meaning and of its *connection* in this Prophetic Moment-in-Time-Prophesied. For the LORD had previously said to me, *"ALL of Time, in the Order of Time and In the Trajectory of Time is speeding up. He who has an ear to hear, let him hear!*

Insights: God's Use Of Earthly Inhabitants...

(As I delivered those words on the Mount of Olives several years ago, there was an enormous clap of thunder—without the benefit of clouds—and the evidence of a Ball of Fire hovered over the Kidron Valley. The grounds shook, the people screamed and I nearly lost my sense of gravity. Additionally, the Lord had said, "There is Power in the Word...Power so strong as to literally burn the atmosphere." Now I was experiencing it!)

Upon our departure from the Tel Aviv Airport, the Prophetic Colors were still at work as the LORD showed me the Blue Colors on the tail of the airplane. Once in the air, He continued to reveal conditions over Israel. He showed me—in an open-eye vision—this scene:

Donkeys and camels were disturbed! I saw the donkeys on a cliff. Their manes were standing up and their nostrils were wide open. Their heads were tossing/threshing about! They were ill-at-ease, prancing and looking in all directions. The camels, too, were upset. They were sensing something in the *air*. Perhaps a blowing of the *winds-of-unrest*, I thought. Then I recognized that this was a moment to TAKE DOMINION and *still* the *winds-of-discord*, In Jesus' Name! "*NOW!*" the LORD exclaimed. And then He continued giving me His insightfulness with instructions/resolutions for the situation:

Pray to still the winds of discord OVER Israel— THIS DAY!

You have lit a candle or TWO. Now light a Prayer or TWO, says the LORD.
The lights are flickering OVER Jerusalem, He said.
Peace accords are broken. Persnickety... Persnickety!" (I understand *persnickety* to mean overly-sensitive, precise or fussy, echoes of discord)
(These letters are again bleeding.)

Back at home there was no rest for me. This vision, and the Work of God for Israel, was not over. The Lord wanted me to comprehend many things so that I might further the Work of His Hands with the full understanding and appreciation for that which He had done not only in Israel, but also in Cambodia. The required research about everything I could find relative Bethlehem and Jerusalem is too enormous for inclusion in this writing. However, I found major correlations to End-Time Prophesy.

* There are promises, Promises and MORE PROMISES that He will Manifest His Presence in Jerusalem.
* It is the *Place* of many things, including the New Jerusalem where no electric lights, or the sun, will be needed.
* It IS and shall ever BE the Eternal Capitol!
* Bethlehem, then, is the City of His Virgin Birth and is recognized as such.

Surely He will display His Presence and Dominion over Jerusalem and EVERYWHERE!

Insights: God's Use Of Earthly Inhabitants...

AN INDIGO ANOINTING HAS BEEN RELEASED

The LORD revealed to me that He had released this *special anointing* that He called an *Indigo Anointing* over Bethlehem and Jerusalem, just as he had over **Cambodia**. The release over Israel was for the Nation, while the release over Cambodia was a release over the *heads* of the *people*. This *Indigo-Glow* in Cambodia was reflected as blue, fine graphite-like crystals which were released like Manna from Heaven, but it *glowed* in the night—in the DARK!

> The LORD accomplishes
> His objectives
> While using different
> Soldiers-of-the-Cross!

✳ The Lord revealed that: *They don't know that it is covering them, any more than they understand the concept of grace and mercy, which is covering them even in their ignorance of the Gospel.*

✳ *The Indigo Anointing is a Provision for a Nation,* says the LORD. *It is a Provision for a Nation! It is the color of Blue-Violet—for Love, Peace, Salvation and <u>Rest</u> from struggles and contention.*

(These colors are manifesting right now—in this writing.)

Insights: God's Use Of Earthly Inhabitants...

The first time that the LORD manifested Himself in an *Indigo Anointing* was several years prior to this trip—just before He sent me to Cambodia in 2001. He visited me and taught me about this special anointing—showing me a scene in Cambodia where I had never been—the same exact scene that I would go to and see later in real life!

Upon my arrival, He sent me into the rice paddies to *Release this Anointing* upon the people. It was awesome and strange. I had never heard of an *Indigo Anointing* before, but in obedience I went and Executed His Plan according to His Will.

Then, <u>exactly</u> five years later—just after my husband passed—the Lord <u>mandated</u> that I *return to Cambodia* with another mission team with whom I had never traveled.

(Colors are now bleeding RED!)

God was now ready to open minds and open doors through this Missions Team! What a Blessing! Upon our arrival, I discovered that the LORD had opened the doors for the first time in this region to allow for public outdoor crusades and Healing Services! When I was in Cambodia before, we met in a room every morning at five o'clock to pray for Open Doors. This time—five years later—this new Ministry Team and I met in the **same room** for breakfast and for Morning Prayers of **Praise**! The doors in Cambodia were now opened, this Ministry Team obeyed God, completed their assign-

Insights: God's Use Of Earthly Inhabitants...

ments, and God truly Blessed the people of Cambodia. They were <u>saved, healed</u> and <u>liberated</u> in Jesus' Name!

In our natural world, a soldier does not an Army make! A nation needs an Army of many skilled warriors from different divisions of service. In the spiritual world of warfare and serving as a Soldier-of-the-Cross, the same truth remains. Each Servant-Soldier is significant to the strategic plans of the Commander-in-Chief. Each is identified by name and number according to your station and assignment.

We need to know our *station* and *assignment* while on duty. And, most importantly, we must honor *Leadership Positions* of our divinely directed connections, while serving in God's Army.

In Congo, Africa

TO **BE** A SERVANT OF THE KING we must *count the cost* and BE READY to walk in the Place-of-Obedience, even as we sometimes hope and pray for a *Ram* in the bushes of our assignments. This is indeed a walk of Faith, as did Abraham and others in their days of service to the King! At this place, one should be ready to learn many lessons, including the lesson of Obedience and Faith-in-Action to an extent not yet tested, in our lives!

During a Women's Conference, several years ago, I was slain by the Holy Spirit! The place where my body landed was right across the Altar, at the point where the body of one who has died, would lay *in state* during funeral services. I knew where I was, but I didn't know why. I laid there so long, that other Ministers came and checked on me from time to time.

I could not move my body, but my mind was most active! I was suspended somewhere in another world, where I saw beautiful, pure white, twinkling lights, which I had never seen before! This experience was

Insights: God's Use Of Earthly Inhabitants...

too comprehensive to explain at this writing, but for the purpose of clarity, I will tell you that I wanted to understand what was happening. So I said: "LORD, I sense that You want something of me. What do You want me to do for You?"

After that experience, I diligently sought for understanding of that which I had seen and heard, but I would not find it until I was ready to die-to-self, and everybody else, for the Cause of Christ. It was in that *place of dying* that I could BE the *true servant* of The King! Over the years, I have come to know not only the depths of that word—BE—but I have come to know much more of Him and His Ways!

The cost of *BEING* in this Place with God cannot be pre-determined. Therefore, the Servant must be so yielded, so trusting and in the state-of-readiness that we are prepared to say, "I have no choice but His. I have no *will* but His!"

> The LORD said:
> *IN THIS HOUR,*
> *I DON'T SEEK SOMEONE WHO WILL DO.*
> *I SEEK SOMEONE WHO WILL BE!*

In Psalms 40:8, David said: "I delight to do Your will, O my God...." While David made that declara-

Insights: God's Use Of Earthly Inhabitants...

---

tion, it is quite another thing to be <u>all</u> that God wants us to *be* while *doing* that which He sends us to <u>do</u> to represent Him before rebellious man!

In this world of ours today He wants us to BE *Ambassadors* for Christ. There are times when He wants us to BE: Saviors and Healers, Peacemakers and Deliverers, and Lovers of the disenfran-  chised, lost and lonely. He wants us to BE Soldiers in the Army of God! BE Defenders of the Causes of Christ, everywhere! And yet, there are many times when it is most difficult to BE *who* the Lord would have us BE.

In 2002 I had such an occasion, when God instructed me to *GO to CONGO, AFRICA!* He had been preparing me for five years for Mission work with an emphasis on Africa. And yet, the hour of His choosing to send me to Congo, Africa, couldn't have been worse—so I thought! Nothing seemed right or orderly. I was feeling terrible about leaving my husband, who was ill and in fact was in the Hospital when I departed for Africa. But, what I didn't understand was that this was the provision that God had made for his care while I was gone! How strange this seemed, and yet My Lord was not releasing me from my assignment to go to Congo, Africa! When you are in the Army of the Lord, You are IN the <u>Army</u>! You are not on furlough. You see, I was on duty in Congo, Africa and my Commander-in-Chief would not release me! These too are the Ways of God!

Insights: God's Use Of Earthly Inhabitants...

I was being sent on an *Africa for Jesus Mission* which was in Kinshasa, Congo, Africa, and I didn't want to go! I saw the need, but I didn't want to BE the one sent! I *wanted* to BE obedient, *IF*.... However, God refused to release me, although I tried to compel Him to do so, with <u>my</u> wisdom thinking.

I was concerned that I would face much persecution from family and friends who did not believe that God would send me away in the midst of my circumstances. I dreaded the hardships to BE contended with once we arrived there and I didn't see how I could put my home affairs in order, sufficiently for my comfort, while going. You see, I had <u>serious</u> worldly cares! My husband was ill; I had no one to care for him in his unhealthy condition! What was I to do? Surely, God is a caring God! So <u>why</u> is He sending me so far away, at this time of my husband's heart failure condition? I knew that a good Soldier must endure hardship! But <u>what about my husband's care</u> while I am gone? And, <u>who</u> will believe that I am walking in *obedience* to God, and not in my own selfishness? I knew that disobedience was not an option! So, I purposed in my heart to walk in obedience, all the while praying for my own *ram-in-the-bushes*. <u>I needed that ram</u>!

> **HAVE NO DOUBTS!**
> **GOD WILL CONFIRM HIS WORD TO YOU**

Insights: God's Use Of Earthly Inhabitants...

Confirmation #1

During this period of indecision, I was mindful that this is a *Suffering-Way!* After all, I had experienced much hardship; adversity was no stranger to me. Besides, I was also remembering a previous occasion. When I was at a point of indecision the LORD would often say: **You take care of My business; I will take care of yours!**

Sometimes I would ask: "LORD, You have shown me this *way* before, but what am I to do now?" He would say: *Oh...just pick up your cross and follow me!*

At this same time, I was also remembering 2 Timothy 2:1-4 which says:

*You therefore, My son, be strong in the grace that is in Christ Jesus. And the things that you have heard from Me among many witnesses, commit these to faithful men who will be able to teach others also. You therefore must endure hardship as a good **soldier** of Jesus Christ. No one engaged in warfare entangles himself with the affairs of this life, that he may please Him who enlisted him as a soldier.*

As the Lord began to deal with me—His *servant-soldier*—very quickly my preparations became more and more intense, with strange words of Prophetic Instructions, which I was required to write! He said to me:

LINKAGE. Linkage—this is about Linkage to My People, My suffering and confused People! Go ahead, trust Me, your Keeper of Dreams and Hopes.

This journey of Hope is overdue. You know that, in your heart-of-hearts, The Word must go forth! The Seeds of Hope must be sown, lest there be no fruit. Remember? Give Me fruit for labor and labor for fruit of My Vine. This is the <u>Love Place</u>. It will do you well.

Preference. Preference. Hallow and sound will teach you when wisdom abounds. <u>Preference</u> is sketchy and tight. It is the favor with Right! Right Message. Right Spirit. Right Order. Right Power. Right Privilege.

Carry the Chamber of My Love with you! Pour it out! Just Pour it out!

I Bless you! Comfort you; Comfort You! Comfort you!

I Praise you, Lord! (I said).

No, I praise you, says the Lord.

Many songs of praise await you. You just give it back to Me! With joy and delight, you give it back—to Me!

Confirmation #2

As I pondered these words/thoughts, I received a phone call from a Prophetic Intercessor, who said: "Turn on your Fax machine. I have a Word for you. This Word is for you, Mary!"

This is the Prophetic word given to her:

"The Prophetic Word—GO! Go! In the Power of My Love and Peace, go! Go! In the Power of My Holy Spirit, I breathe upon you—Go! You ask Me where, but you know where I beckon. You know where I call. You know your Master's voice!

You are my sheep whom I have set apart; whom I have taught. I trained you in the rocky places. I trained you in the mountain regions. I trained you in the storms of the seas. I trained you for the battlefield. I TRAINED YOU WITH MY OWN HAND!

I moved in the depths of your heart, and I cleaned out that which was not needed for war. I molded you with My own HANDS, and I shaped you for such a TIME AS THIS! A TIME OF WAR! There is WAR on the earth, and there is WAR in the heavenlies. Stand Tall! The T-I-M-E has come. YES, the T-I-M-E is even NOW!

Insights: God's Use Of Earthly Inhabitants...

Your Preparation, your time of Drought, your Time of Desert, Your Time of Tears, was for THIS TIME—MY TIME! The TIME IS NOW!

Be still and hear the thunder in the skies. My Angels are troops that are ready for battle. Tune your ears. You know My Voice. It is the Voice Who calls you from your slumber in the midnight hours of war, in prayer. It is the Voice Who calls you from the silence of your pain, to Love as I Love—To Love Now! Love those who hurt you, even as I Loved you from the beginning of TIME!

It is My Voice that calls you to Heal in My Name and See My Power when you Just Let Me BE God. You are My Tool. I LEAD YOU—One, one WAY, One another WAY. I will not call you all into the same place of war. I will not empower you all with the same gifts. But where I lead, you will go in victory! I have conquered! I have the victory!

I HAVE TRAINED YOU FOR THIS TIME—THIS TIME OF WAR! GO! GO, where I send you and DO NOT look back. For it is FORWARD that you go! Forward! FORWARD! Marching to WAR!

Hold HIGH your banner that proclaims MY NAME—and GO!"

Confirmation #3

THEN, MY LORD SENT yet another messenger with Prophetic words of courage for me. This is what he heard from the LORD:

"The Victory has already been WON, but you have to GO to the PLACE of the victory in order to receive the Victory Won, and the Victory Promised. The LORD has accomplished the warfare. He has won the Victory. YOU have to GO TO IT! You have to go to the Victory-Place which has been won."

Confirmation #4, 5, 6, 7...

THEN, by further illumination, the LORD revealed His deeper *purpose* for me during this trip. I was going to Proclaim His Love—given to them—and to <u>claim</u> and <u>proclaim</u> Africa for Jesus, teaching as I went along that it's a Highway to Heaven (for the *pure in heart* to walk there)!

To propel me toward my destiny, God began to give me Supernatural Signs. First I saw the word *Time* being written in the heavenlies! Then repeatedly I was shown the clock. Each time it would be 10:10 O'clock.

> Light-balls appeared to drop down into place in the darkness then stop suddenly until the message IT IS TIME, was spelled out in the skies.

Insights: God's Use Of Earthly Inhabitants...

Then, 11:11 O'clock, until I was convinced that God was up to something "Wondrous!

Later I found out that we were to depart for our *Africa for Jesus Mission* in Congo, Africa, on the 11th Month, 10th day, 2002 at 10:00 P.M., in order to be at our destination on the 11th month, 11th day 2002 at 11:00 O'clock AM.

Ten (10) is the Prophetic number for *order* in Governments. Our Mission would include Ministry at the Palace, where I delivered my first prophetic words to the Nation. Relative to the number Eleven (11), the LORD had previously said that we are...

* ❋ *In the Eleventh Hour of the Prophetic Clock of Time.*
* ❋ *There is but a Moment of Time left on the Prophetic Clock of Time for this generation*
* ❋ *And that All of Time is speeding up in the Trajectory-of-Time!*

> You see, God communicates His Will to us by many means, including:
> Messengers of God and the God-Kind, Prophetic Numbers, Prophetic Colors, Prophetic Words, and Signs and Wonders!

Satan also has a parallel of prophetic counterfeit numbers. He has a Counter Plan to God's and he will

Insights: God's Use Of Earthly Inhabitants...

also try to show you counterfeit signs. In this case he tried many tactics. For example: On November 1, 2002, AT 10:10 P.M. (ten days before my departure), I admitted my husband into the hospital—with pneumonia—where he stayed for five (5) days. Then he came home! Two days later, I re-admitted him, for observation, and he would stay there for the duration of my Mission trip, plus two more days after my return. In the midst of it all, God was still in control, with His ram-in-the-bushes of my concerns!

You see, during my absence, the Doctors decided to go ahead and put in a heart pacemaker, which had been pre-determined useful for his medical condition. After the procedure, my husband needed two extra days in the hospital, before he was released to come home. This gave me two days to rest after my 30,000 mile trip. I was quite tired upon my return, and thankful for the brief rest afforded.

PROPHETIC MOMENT AT THE PALACE, KINSHASA, AFRICA

**Prophetic Sound-bites of HOPE for Congo—A Nation in Despair
Tell Them To Prepare for Revival
Tell Them To Prepare to Disciple Souls**

I mmediately upon arrival at the airport in Kinshasa, Capitol of Congo, Africa we began to encounter opposition and chaos ensued! The lights went out at the Airport, confusion followed and it became fearsome, to say the least! The situation became sufficiently serious and internationally embarrassing to warrant an Official Invitation to The Palace for an Official Apology—two days later! The graciousness of the Governmental hospitality extended to us, lasted for the duration of our visitation! Our Lord and Savior used this event for His own Glory!

    The Lord had given me a Prophetic *Word of Hope* before departing the United States of America, but

Insights: God's Use Of Earthly Inhabitants...

I had no idea how, or to whom, I would deliver it! THEN my Lord opened the doors of the Palace, through these scary experiences, and I delivered that *Message of Hope* to the People by way of the Official Press, which had been summoned to interview us!

During the delivery of those Prophetic *Words of Hope*, on the lawn of the Flower Gardens, the Holy Spirit engulfed me and I could feel the ground moving under my feet in all directions! I had never experienced such movement, nor had I felt such a surge of electric currents through my body! As I heard my own words pour forth from my mouth, my ears couldn't believe! <u>I was not in control;</u> The Holy Spirit was in control and the staff knew it!

The audience began to respond with amazement and bewilderment! One person came immediately to me, for healing. Without delay, I prayed for her and no one seemed to object. Someone called out asking: "Where is she getting these words she speaks?" "She has no notes!" Then, I heard someone answer saying, *"It is just coming out of her belly!"*

Two days later, I was taken back to the Palace to meet with our hosting Official who told me that, from my previously recorded *Prophetic Message,* **"Sound Bites of Hope"** would be prepared for airing—over TV and radio stations—to encourage the People of Congo who sorely needed encouragement, and that the airing of the Message would continue long after I had returned to the United Stated!

We received much Official favor throughout our stay! They even accompanied us to the Airport for our departure home! Isn't God Amazing!!!

ANOTHER PROPHETIC WORD

On November 12, 2002, at 5 A.M., the day after our arrival in Congo, the Lord gave me another *Prophetic Word* for the Ministry Servants. (It was a Twenty-One Points of Wisdom Message at five o'clock A.M. The Prophetic Five [5] represents Mercy and Grace and the Twenty-one [21] is also a Prophetic number, divisible by three and seven—3=invincibility; 7=sovereignty.)

"Tell them to prepare for Revival. Prepare to Disciple the souls. Expect the outpouring of the many gifts within the Body. It is the season of need for servants in the Kingdom. The Prophets shall spring forth as waters breaking—birthing My Causes! This is a New Day upon the earth. I have need of you, My Servants. Come forth into My Service. Yield and will your wills to Me, The Mighty One! I will prepare you and make you in the likeness of Myself. I will equip you with the Power of My Might! I will equip you with the Power of My Release for you, so that—so that— SO THAT ye shall BE Empowered FOR Service! I will RELEASE My very presence among you— and show you things which you know not! I will show you the phenomenal thing upon the EARTH in this Time and Season," says the Lord.

Insights: God's Use Of Earthly Inhabitants...

"Expectancy. Expectancy is Key and importantly essential in this hour of need! There is Power in expectancy! Expect Me to show up and RELEASE MY Love—My Love for Correction, Adjustment and Salvation. I Am a God of Love! Hear Me! I know that which is best for you and for your African Nation! Trust Me to do you Good—Not Harm. For I Am Your God...Your Lord...Your Savior...Your Peace!" says the Lord.

Hear Me! Hear Me! Receive My Instructions to you—For your Liberation—For your Correction! says the Lord.

THE LORD AGAIN SHOWED HIMSELF MIGHTY!

He opened the doors to the Cathedral, and I delivered His Message at High Noon! (Twelve [12] represents the *completeness* or *wholeness* of divine and human relationship under Creator God.)

We would discover later that the President was actively engaged in a Peace-Seeking Plan among rivaling factions which had found no means to be at Peace for generations. It was thought by other Nations to be a futile attempt, especially for this, the youngest of all Presidents universally. They did find a Peace formula, though fragile! As they struggled and worked toward a peaceful existence, we continued to pray and to put trust in the Prophetic words of Hope which the LORD gave to me for them!

FOUR YEARS LATER

It is four (4) years later, November 14, 2006, to the exact date of our presence in Congo, Africa, when the Lord said to me, *I Am still dealing with the number FOUR (4).*

I didn't understand the statement—although I knew the number four to represent worldwide impact—until the next morning when I saw the *Washington Post* Newspaper Headlines: "INCUMBENT DECLARED WINNER IN CONGO VOTE." The article, by Stephanie McCrummen, Washington Post Foreign Services reporter, reads:

> Kinshasa, Congo, November 15, 2006... "Incumbent Joseph Kabila was on Wednesday declared the winner of Congo's first presidential elections in more than 40 years, as the crumbling boulevards of the capital remained calm.
>
> "Mr. Kabila, who took power after his father, Laurent Kabila, was assassinated in 2001, faces the challenges of satisfying the high expectations of the electorate, including the 42 percent who voted for Mr. Jean-Pierre Bemba, in a country of 200 ethnic groups and at least that many political parties," writes Ms. McCrummen.
>
> President Kabila takes charge of a country still imbued with the legacy of its longtime dictator, Mobutu Sese Seko, who looted <u>billions</u> from the government during his 32-year

rule. The violence, disease and famine accompanying the civil war that followed, left more than 4 million people dead!"

(Basically everyone is expecting a change in this country. But, we must pray for good, organized, patient change, without more fighting and loss of life! There are about 32 million people in this counties population. Foreign donors poured out $450 million to support the vote, but this is a delicate, complicated process of democracy. Eighty percent of the population is unemployed! As of September, 2010, Kabila is still in office. This President needs a mature, political culture, for it is effectively a cultural war to change things for the better in this country. Let us pray, DILIGENTLY!)

And now you see, My Beloveds, another example of how the LORD utilizes His *Earthly Inhabitants—* HIS *CHANGE AGENTS.* Even as current assignments end we must continue to Fast and Pray without ceasing—and remember the Promises of Hope. Hold fast to them!! There is Hope! There IS God! And, there are the Righteous Servants whom the LORD hears when we intercede for the Nations who have suffered for so long!

THE PRESENCE OF GOD IN CHINA

PROPHET ON ASSIGNMENT

Now in these latter years of my *service*—October, 2009—the Lord revealed Himself yet again to be *Sovereign Lord* during the first Government-sanctioned Open Healing Service in Kunming, China! He allowed me to be there as a living witness—a *God-moment* in my life—a true Landmark-in-Time! Even though I've been blessed with many divine experiences and encounters, these events became incredibly amazing lessons demonstrating and including the intervention of Angels and works of the Holy Spirit. As I share with you my reflections and revelations of that which the LORD has done during this Historic Mission/Ministry, please observe the **process** of His Ways to Victory— His Divine Strategies for *Setting Captives Free*!

I offer more specific details in this Chapter so that you will know of the Lord's intimate involvement with His Causes; **how** He blends uniquely positioned ministry teams for His Purposes; and so that you might more clearly see and discover the Lord's *Building Blocks* of Servant-hood in your own development.

Insights: God's Use Of Earthly Inhabitants...

THE LORD HAS NOT CLOSED HIS HEART TO CHINA

For many, many centuries, Missionaries have traveled to China. Some have lost their lives for this Cause of Christ! This was my third Mission to China, and by God's Amazing Grace, I was privileged to travel with a minister who has made <u>forty</u> visits there.

In the creation of the heavens and the earth—and all that dwells therein—God was Strategically Methodical. There was preparation for man before He created Adam, then Eve, and the two set the course for all of humanity. The Lord, God has not changed! He is <u>methodical</u> [orderly] and <u>strategic</u> [deliberate] in what He does whether in a human person or within a *Nation Cause* affecting many people. And, so it is that we observe the Processes, Strategies, and Methodology—applied God's Way—to the Mission Causes in China.

> Our God is strategic and methodical In all that He does.

There is also *Pre-requisite Readiness* on the part of the *Sent-Servant*. Personally, spiritually and in every other aspect of life's planning, *readiness* is required. For me, I needed to understand <u>why</u> I must go to China—for <u>what</u> purpose—and <u>why now</u>? Please *know* that God is Faithful to give His instructions in all the areas of one's life, including the assurance that you are, indeed, *sent* and that <u>this is your set time to go</u>! In this current experience, the LORD assured

Insights: God's Use Of Earthly Inhabitants...

me of my assignment, time and purpose saying: *You must go to some places that others cannot. This is your SET TIME to the NATIONS. Ascribe your mind to this Truth.* With that understanding, I moved forward to make ready for this assigned work. As mentioned before, the Lord directed me to read Psalm 96 multiple times. I include it here for your edification.

Oh, sing to the LORD a new song!
Sing to the LORD, all the earth.
Sing to the LORD, bless His name;
Proclaim the good news of His salvation
from day to day.
Declare His glory among the nations,
His wonders among all peoples.
For the LORD *is* great and greatly to be praised;
He *is* to be feared above all gods.
For all the gods of the peoples *are* idols,
But the LORD made the heavens.
Honor and majesty *are* before Him;
Strength and beauty *are* in His sanctuary.
Give to the LORD, O families of the peoples,
Give to the LORD glory and strength.
Give to the LORD the glory *due* His name;
Bring an offering, and come into His courts.
Oh, worship the LORD in the beauty of holiness!
Tremble before Him, all the earth.
Say among the nations, "The LORD reigns;
The world also is firmly established,
It shall not be moved;
He shall judge the peoples righteously."
Let the heavens rejoice, and let the earth be glad;

Let the sea roar, and all its fullness;
Let the field be joyful, and all that *is* in it.
Then all the trees of the woods will
rejoice before the Lord.
For He is coming, for He is coming to
judge the earth.
He shall judge the world with righteousness,
And the peoples with His truth.

My further personal preparation included: diet adjustments, health and fitness, appropriate clothing, and Prophetic Attire—garments to be worn at the appointed time according to God's divine instruction. And, of course, Spiritual readiness was of paramount importance, highest on the list of priorities. There was an urgent need to *activate* the Intercessors—those who would cover me and the Missions Team in *prayer*. As I contacted them, I specifically asked for prayers to **guard** the God-Purposes in me as I set forth to walk in His Will and His Ways while completing my assigned tasks!

(Prophetic Guard: is the term given for shielding of spiritual forces that Prophets emit in order to deflect the assaults and stratagems that devils throw at the people of God. Prophets guard, pray, intercede and compel provision to be manifested and enforce New Testament/Christ's Cross-offerings of obedience, upon the forces of darkness!)

Insights: God's Use Of Earthly Inhabitants...

Realizing that the task before us was enormous, I quickly mobilized seven hundred (700) radical-faith, Christian Believers, Prayer Warrior/Intercessors who possessed a co-laboring spirit for this Cause of Christ in China.

Angelic Assistance in China

HEAR THIS! The date was September 10, 2009 (9-10-09 at 9 AM)—a little over a month before our trip would begin. Suddenly, CHINA was in my foremost vision as the Holy Spirit descended upon me, mightily.

Then, I heard the LORD say:

My Spirit has gone before you this day!

Heaven had dispatched the *ANGELIC EAGLE* to China in preparation for our mission. This bird-like Angel was <u>enormous</u> and <u>strong</u> beyond my ability to describe. However, I observed these features: He was brown in color, likened to an Eagle. His wings were outstretched as he glided gently into his place, which I knew was China. The

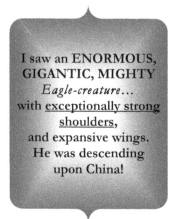

I saw an ENORMOUS, GIGANTIC, MIGHTY *Eagle-creature...* with <u>exceptionally strong shoulders,</u> and expansive wings. He was descending upon China!

Insights: God's Use Of Earthly Inhabitants...

STRENGTH in his shoulders was unmistakable as I observed his landing.

I not only observed and knew many details concerning this Vision, but I felt them throughout my entire being for days. I *knew*—beyond doubt—that the LORD had gone before us that day!

My *assigned readings* were many, but the story of David fighting Goliath with only a staff and his amazing trust in God, was one of them (1 Samuel 17). A companion Scripture was 1 Samuel 10:6-8, encouraging me to *"...do as the occasion demands, for God is with* [me]." Then, as I read Ephesians 1:7-10, I saw the core message that must reach China:

- ➢ IN HIM we have **Redemption** through His Blood.
- ➢ We have ***Forgiveness of sins***...according to His Grace...abounding toward ALL
- ➢ SO THAT, *in the fullness of Time* He might gather together ALL—yes, ALL—things in the Heavens and on the Earth, <u>IN HIM!</u>

Then, as I continued in study and meditation, I saw China's End-Time *role* in History and found much connection to Israel!

I also understood that the Eagle *likeness* represents Freedom and Liberty. The color—brown—represents Warfare and Power. The very <u>strong shoulders</u> represent Divine Strength, and Burden-

Insights: God's Use Of Earthly Inhabitants...

Bearing Capacity. The Prophetic numbers—nine and ten—represent New Birth Timing (9), and God's Governmental Order (10). And, throughout the following days (and nights) the Lord continued to pour more insights into me.

THEN, just a few days before departure, I woke experiencing tearful, painful eyes. I couldn't imagine what was happening. I kept going to the mirror to see if I had a red-eye condition, but my eyes were clearer than usual! Later that day as I was reading/researching I learned of the health conditions in China—13 million Chinese are blind! Immediately, I submitted my prayer request to the Intercessors—for a Special Anointing for *eyes* during this Mission to China.

Observe: The Prophet's Journey
The Process to Victory and the Lord's Horsemen Sent Into Battle

There is the *expected*, logistical process of airplane flights from home states to the Mission-Team Assembly Place, in this case, Los Angeles, California. We then flew about <u>fourteen</u> continuous hours before arriving in Hong Kong. From there we boarded connecting flights to Beijing—Wuhan—Shanghai—and finally Kunming where the Healing Services were convened. Then, of course, we reversed this process in order to return home, complete with yet more Immigration and official checkpoints before arriving at our home destinations! These are rigorous tasks—blessed of God—**and, yet this too is the required work of ministry to the Nations.**

Following are the highlights of this **journey's** <u>liberating</u> process.

Insights: God's Use Of Earthly Inhabitants...

Day One:

Just after arriving at our hotel, the LORD showed me a HEART—a heart that was CHANGING—as if GROWING A NEW HEART out of the old one. I saw NEW GROWTH coming forth upon a heart!

I began to pray as I was concerned that someone among us might be experiencing a heart problem! I prayed diligently about that which I saw, as I initially thought the vision to be of a natural heart! Soon, I received revelation and understood this vision to represent the *Heartlands of China*.

Day Three:

I received a divine visitation—with revelations— about that which would be accomplished through *Prophetic Acts* at a <u>bridge</u>. This work required great faith. The Lord had taught me His ways for **hours** during the night, only to hear <u>the same message being taught the next morning by our anointed, Apostolic Teacher and Mission Leader</u>. The focus of that morning message was ***Faith in Process***, and the main points were: Faith is NOW; There Are *Measures* of Faith; and STAY in the Process.

During the night vision, I tried to show the works (Prophetic Acts) to others but they could not see it. So they did not believe! The LORD began to speak of those who must *see* to believe, saying:

Oh, ye of little faith! You have NOT Believed that I AM! OH, ye of <u>Little Faith</u>!

Oh, ye of Great Faith—HOLD ON to your Dreams for My Beloved China—Personalized! MY CHINA! MY CHINA! SHE IS MINE! I WOO HER...even as I woo you!

It was then 4:45 AM and the Lord began to speak more saying: *A NEW DAY IS DAWNING! Prepare yourself for the Breakthrough! It will be GREAT! Expect great transformations to take place. BE GRATEFUL FOR MY LOVE!*

Then, a <u>Prophetic Song</u> came forth in my spirit and eventually out of my mouth:

A NEW DAY IS DAWNING...CAN YOU SEE IT?
A NEW DAY IS DAWNING, CAN YOU FEEL IT?
A NEW WAY IS DAWNING, CAN YOU BELIEVE IT?
IT'S <u>BLOWING</u> IN THE <u>WIND</u>, MY FRIEND
THE <u>ANSWER</u> MY FRIEND, IS <u>BLOWING IN</u>
<u>THE WIND</u>
*THE **<u>ANSWER</u>** IS BLOWING IN THE WIND!*
Waters are flowing...
Winds are blowing...
The answer My friend is blowing in the Wind!
Mercy...Mercy...Mercy....MERCY

The word, *Mercy,* was repeated over and over again four times. Each time He spoke the word *ANSWER,* He placed more emphasis on the word by elongating or stretching the word out, for emphasis. These words/verses were repeated in my soul for hours! Then, I had to sing the words out loud, proclaiming His words! Soon, other Ministers who trav-

Insights: God's Use Of Earthly Inhabitants...

eled with me were also singing the melodies with much amazement and with glee!

Day Four:

At 3:00 a.m. the next morning the same Prophetic Song, "A NEW DAY IS DAWNING," resounded in my thoughts over and over again. But then the Lord revealed His Presence/Himself to me in Living Colors—Royal Purple colors! I was awestruck and certain that His Supernatural manifestation—with signs and wonders following—was to be experienced soon! In fact, I was not disappointed and neither was the Missionary team of Servants who were of one accord!

Ministry *Faith* Teachings continued for the Team, followed by Tour Guide-teaching about China's History. We traveled through the Heartlands of China, to the Headlands and through the Agriculture lands (life-sustaining foods for the stomach). I was fully engaged in The Lord's Movement and the execution of His will, as He revealed Himself and directed my activity.

Day Five:

At 5:00 AM the Lord was speaking these words in my ears:

> **The HEALING of the Nations!** *A New Day is sprung from the recesses of the old heart. A New Growth has sprung! I showed it to you in New Concepts related to the Natural man—*

who needed a new heart—NOT a transplanted heart!

A New Growth has come forth bearing children! There are no children to bear the fruit of My blessings released—to bring them into the Promised Land of My Glory Place! THIS MUST CHANGE!

Pray Change—policy change. I saw fit to use My Servant [our leader/host Minister] who had experienced heart issues/conditions. But I gave her heart STRENGTH! SO CAN I GIVE THIS NATION A NEW HEART! From the heart doth flow Rivers of Living Waters of HOPE and PROMISE! A New Heart—A New Nation—A New Birth! Waters are BROKEN! Babies will come forth! It's been a hard labor, He continued.

That night the Ministry Leader taught on the topics of "Healing Strategies" and "Crazy Faith." **And as she spoke I heard the LORD saying:** ***In Jesus' Name, receive a new heart Nation of China!*** I simply agreed with the revealed Will of God, with eager expectation of that which was to become manifested. My heart experienced indescribable joy. We must continue to proclaim a New Heart for China and Speak the Promises/Solutions!

Day Six...

<u>For the third day</u>, at 8:30 AM, the same Prophetic Song was before me: *The answer my friend is blowing in the wind...the answer is blowing in...the wind!* Much emphasis was placed on the words <u>*A-N-S-W-E-R*</u> and

Insights: God's Use Of Earthly Inhabitants...

BLOWING, as the Lord seemed to stretch the words in His speaking them again!

[Dictionary helps for your consideration and reflection:

In the *Strong's Hebrew Dictionary*, the word, ***ANSWER*** (*ANAH*/ עָנָה/aw-naw') means *to speak; specifically to sing, shout, testify, announce...to lift up...bear witness...*

Wind (ruach/וּחַ/ roo'-akh): That which passes quickly, the air put in motion by divine *breath*; inspired, invisible, intangible; the *divine miracle power* by which inanimate things begin to move (Ezekiel 10:17; Zechariah 5:9.) The future empowering of the Messiah (Isaiah 11:2; 42:1; 61:1).

Blow(s) (puach /וּתַּם/poo'akh): To blow with the breath of air; to kindle (a fire); to speak/utter; the arrival and presence of the Spirit Being (John 3:8)]

With this song continuing in my heart and mind, and my expectations building, I discovered that my perception of the mission and ministry of the Angels in God's plans also increased. **Angels** (malak/מַלְאָך/ mal-awk') are divine gifts—ambassadors, messengers, envoys—mightily and strategically used for service, manifested by the *breath* of God (Hebrews 1:14). Angels are sent on assignment for the benefit of man (Ezekiel 9).

Insights: God's Use Of Earthly Inhabitants...

Day Seven...
Wearing of Prophetic Garments was <u>required</u> for this *work* assignment.
BY DIVINE MANDATE this was a day of isolation for me, a day of intimacy with God, and a day of warfare, in readiness for the Historic FIRST Open Healing Service in China, later that night. I was required to wear the distinctive <u>purple</u> satin pajamas that the Lord had told me to take to China and, indeed, I did so—ALL DAY! During this day of intimacy with the Lord (and wearing the assigned purple garment), I felt troubled with the revealed understanding that there were problems related to our Healing Services scheduled that night.

Then, the Lord spoke saying: ***444 HORSEMEN AT YOUR DISPOSAL!***

His announcement required my Prophetic Response to this Revelation.

I said: "Loose them...Position them...I receive them. Lord, You have seen them necessary!"

At this point I understood that His Will was coming forth. These Prophetic words had to be <u>spoken aloud in agreement</u> with the Will of God. **If we don't do our part to release His Will upon the earth, the outcomes will be altered.**

<u>Additional Prophetic Garments Would Be Required</u>
<u>for Readiness and Warfare</u>

While remaining in prayer that day, God instructed me regarding what to wear to the Healing services that night! This article of clothing was a <u>three piece,</u>

Insights: God's Use Of Earthly Inhabitants...

royal purple cotton garment trimmed with gold threads about the neck, wrist of the sleeves, down the front of the jacket and around the bottom of my long skirt.

> The mantle signifies status, authority, and station of the Officer in the Prophetic realms of creation.
> The Heavenly hosts, as well as the demonic, respect these garments in the authority place.

As mentioned earlier, the Old Testament Prophets often wore different garments to distinguish themselves. Today, *Prophetic Attire* is the supernatural clothing of the Prophet that constitutes his or her uniform-of-service. The angelic guard, and demons that oppose them, observe this act of dress. Spiritually speaking, a Prophetic *Mantle* is the term for the *cloak* worn by the Prophets to designate their **authority** in their Community Ministry and in the spirit realm. John the Baptist, Elijah and many other Prophets were recognized by the unique style of the *mantle* they wore.

In the present age these specified garments are worn more for the invisible agents of God's creation than for the people of the earth.

<u>IN REFLECTION</u>: During this time in China, we had One Hundred Eleven (111) Ministers including the Leader, and the Lord provided Heavenly assistance— Four Hundred Forty-Four (444) Horsemen—each of us having Four (4) Horsemen to support us!

Insights: God's Use Of Earthly Inhabitants...

> Spiritually, *HORSEMEN* signify Messengers of Judgment, *SUPERNATURAL PATROL*, and *BATTLE.* (Isaiah 22:6-9.)

> FOUR: The number four (4) represents Divine Intervention (interruption) which spiritually involves the four winds (see note on definition of *wind* above); a Divine *command* that takes in humanity and the entire planet. (Genesis 2:10; Jeremiah 49:36; Ezekiel 1:8; Daniel 7:6; Zechariah 6:5; Acts 10:11)

Day Eight...
The Lord Censures His Servants
For Waste of Resources (and Time)

The LORD'S Heart is turned toward His Children. He spoke to His people through me asking: *FOR WHAT will you deny my children?* For WHAT will you deny MY CHILDREN?

Today's Ministry teachings focused on selfless love and Joshua's successes which were realized as Joshua *spoke* the **Word** day and night. During the previous day of isolation, the Lord spoke to me of *His Children*, and the *squandered resources* on materialistic goods, while the children are denied. He was sharing His heart concerning man's priorities versus His. Listening to this day's message brought much confirmation.

Earth's Timepieces Addressed

The Lord began to reveal His specific concerns relative *Earth's Time Pieces*—expensive watches on

Insights: God's Use Of Earthly Inhabitants...

which man places TOO MUCH money and dependence. He said: *COSTLY Time Pieces you afford yourselves, America, France, and the rest of Ye Ole Nations! Why squander ye resources on that which is NOT BREAD for MY children? In Heaven, all of Heaven's beauty is bread for the children's enjoyment and pleasure. So, what will you do? What will you DO? What will you do with your riches—from the Ashes—Ashes of your hopes dashed—ASHES of banished hopes— real and with sorrows looming overhead? What will you do with the Ashes of pending sorrows looming heavy, even in this hour of seeming prosperity.*

He continued: *Here in this sorrowful land of Myths and Adages there is no TRUE Hope in their hearts. Happiness and laughter does not equate with the TRUTH of Eternal JOY!*

Earth's timepieces have become OBSOLETE in the REAL sense! Morning, evening—night and day—it cannot tell.

THEN the Lord showed me a multitude of rich, diamond-studded watches—valuable to man—but of NO VALUE in Heaven. (And as I write this, I am reminded of my experience when the Lord translated me to heaven where I was shown His children playing with earth's expensive watches in the beautiful *diamond-studded **sand*** along Heaven's path. The children were freely and joyously playing with *diamonds*, all sizes and shapes of sparkling diamonds mixed among the sand. I was told that watches have no purpose there, and that time is not measured as it is on earth.)

Insights: God's Use Of Earthly Inhabitants...

Day Nine...
INSIGHTS Into Multi-Dimensional Impacts:
Thy Will Be Done On Earth—As In Heaven
Accomplished by the Strategies of God

This day's Ministry Message to the Team was titled ONE BOAT and encouraged us that Faith and Obedience are needed to fulfill our <u>Destiny Process</u> (Luke 5:1-11... *Launch out into the deep and let down your nets for a catch*). Natural reasoning will cause us to miss our moment(s). Blessings come through a PROCESS of OBEDIENCE.

Later that day, in Shanghai, we saw China's *Equator*—their Economic and Financial Trade Center. Shanghai's growth, from rice paddies to mega metropolis in 18 years, <u>includes myths regarding the number eight (8).</u> Eight is their present mythical guiding number—which means Money to them—I was told. So they build eight bridges, eight tunnels, eight high speed Metro Train Lines etc. China's former guiding number for the Nation was number nine (9) representing longevity, happiness, good luck, etc. But, note, that has <u>changed</u> to the importance of MONEY in their lives. Now, they perceive that Money is the answer to their problems.

Spiritually, number eight (8) represents NEW BEGINNINGS. Also, the number eighteen (18) in Hebrew represents *LIFE*. Biblically, nine (9) represents gestation, birth, new life, maturity. But the Chinese think of the number 9 as **good luck,** happiness and longevity—which is a reflection of the error of Spiritual and mental perception. **There are**

Insights: God's Use Of Earthly Inhabitants...

---

perceptions and there are <u>truths</u> **to be told and revealed; you see!** There are also mysterious elements of the unknown operating in the world. This enigmatic state of affairs needs to be corrected, by someone! It will not happen without yielded Truth-seeking and Truth-defending Servants!

Day Nine and Ten...

The Dawning of a New Day and of Deliverance had arrived! This Team of Ministers began the First Historic **Open** Healing Services in China— our blessed privilege—an amazing occasion! The Presence of the Lord was there! He blessed mightily through His corporate anointing and He used His Servant-Leaders with great wisdom.

Fortified by the Holy Spirit's Words of Knowledge, **many were healed of Eye conditions,** bone conditions and of inner woundedness! As tears of true joy, wet the faces of the Chinese people, they embraced us with loving embraces! This then, became our moment to minister by the laying-on of our hands upon them, for more healing experiences, and for more opportunities to impart to this Nation God's Love toward them!

We Proclaimed the Victory and gave All Glory to our GOD—To Him Who Manifested His Dynamic Life-Changing Power through...

    ❋ DIVINE INTERVENTION that set the PROCESS in ACTION

Insights: God's Use Of Earthly Inhabitants...

* The Host of Heaven sent to China before us, in the image of an enormous Eagle/Angel with exceptional strength in his Wings at the shoulder—burden-bearing place!
* The Power of the Preached Word and the Power of the Proclaimed Word—working the Will of God—as Victory was realized!
* The fervent prayers of the ministry team sent up to the Lord by Day and by Night
* The *execution* of His Will released through...
  - o Prophetic Acts
  - o Prophetic Songs
  - o The Presence of powerful Angels
  - o The Dispatch of 444 Horsemen (divine/ supernatural warriors)—which were at our disposal as they intervened and went to war during contentious times which threatened the Cause of Christ in China.
  - o **There was manifestation of many people Healed and Saved—Captives were set free!**
  - o **AND we won favor with the Chinese Government Officials who have expressed their wishes for MORE such services in the future.**

This was a Momentous and Historic Breakthrough!

THIS TIME OF MINISTRY had not only been a Vision seen, but had become a Vision AND a Promise in the PROCESS!

Insights: God's Use Of Earthly Inhabitants...

In a Nation where for centuries Freedom, Liberty and Justice has been denied, Our Lord demonstrated His Sovereignty while using His servants in many different ways to set the captives free!

Day Twelve...

Back in the United States, my heart and mind was still in China! Apparently, the Lord's heart was still in China as well since He was speaking much about this Nation which He proclaimed to BE HIS! Throughout the many days in China, we spent much time together and He spoke, saying these Words:

> *WHY lay up for yourselves treasures on Earth—indeed! Many yokes need to be broken in this stronghold of ideas, held in error. BREAK THEM! FREE THEM! The Strongman is over them! SETTING THE CAPTIVES FREE IS A WORK OF MY HAND THROUGH YOU! SEE?*
>
> *CAPTIVITY IS EVERYWHERE! It applies to nations and to man. Nations of peoples suffer captivity of mind and of circumstances. ALL are included in the works of your hands, as I guide them to perform.* (He encouraged).

The Lord then began to teach me more about Prophetic Garments, saying: *GARMENTS WORN MUST SPEAK MY MOVEMENT,* as He caused me to reflect on the **Prophetic Garments of Color** which He had mandated that I wear on specific days. The colors were of **Olive Green, Purple, Brown** (likened to the Eagle Creature which was sent before us), <u>and</u>

Insights: God's Use Of Earthly Inhabitants...

A Scarf of many colors, with two Peacocks of Gold and Silver threads on each end. The two very ornate peacock designs are made of flowers and stitched in their places inside revolving doors. One is of Purple highlights; the other is made of gold and silver colors. They are very elegant and beautiful birds— birds of beauty, not birds of war—birds of freedom and liberty!

He also brought again to my remembrance THE EAGLE—the prophetic symbol of spiritual and divine omniscience and victory! Eagles are also equated with spiritual quickening and renovation. They tend to their young as extraordinary nurturers, and are meticulous about the development of their young. Ezekiel Chapter One pictures them as Eternal, *living* beings, part of a dynamic revelation, and Job 39:27 presents them as very responsive to the voice of Creator God. These are the characteristics one finds in *genuine* prophets!

> Through it all...
> I continue to count it
> ALL JOY
> TO SERVE THE LORD;
> To be in His service
> In the Office of Prophet
> and Called to the Nations!

THEN, during another early morning hour, in spite of my fatigue, He caused me to *LAUGH* and *LAUGH*, and *LAUGH out LOUD*—with an unspeakable JOY! THAT TOO WAS AMAZING!

Insights: God's Use Of Earthly Inhabitants...

Later, as I gathered my mail, the <u>FORTUNE MAGAZINE</u> was there awaiting my return, with an article on China. On its front cover was a picture of a RED SHOPPING BAG, made of a Chinese flag, complete with its five stars. Amazingly, **the big bag was filled with global earth**, and with room to spare. The Magazine's heading reads: CHINA BUYS THE WORLD: ITS CHINA'S WORLD. WE JUST LIVE IN IT.

Bill Powell, the writer, had written an extensive article about "China and her ability to purchase the World" with her BOUNTY OF MONEY. His Title: CHINA BUYS THE WORLD was an attention-getter for me. He stated: "The Chinese have long been on a shopping spree for natural resources. NOW, with $2 Trillion in their pockets, they are shifting their aim toward Auto-Makers, High Tech Firms, Real Estate and more. Where will China's present and future global position in the world take us? Leave us?"

<u>Years ago, the Lord said to me that China had been marginalized.</u>

I found the *Fortune Magazine* article amazingly insightful and timely in its publication and there have now been other such articles continuing to ask pertinent questions. I sensed that God was still proving His constant Sovereignty over the world! Perhaps China will be marginalized no more...nor will she be in an enigmatic state relative the power of Jesus and His shed blood on the cross.

Insights: God's Use Of Earthly Inhabitants...

As I've continued to reflect and share quiet time with the Lord, He has shown me that...

* ❋ Because someone **yielded the Will of God** for China;
* ❋ **Because someone answered the call to Go;**
* ❋ **Because someone stepped forward to BE the one who would walk in obedience to execute His will,** as His Inhabitants or Vessels in the Earth;
* ❋ **Because someone willingly** yielded **everything** for His Kingdom purposes...

...perhaps China will be *Marginalized No More* in relation to other nations—nor will she continue in her *Enigmatic State-of mind* relative **to the Truth** and the Power of the Cross—the **FREE GIFT** afforded for salvation, and for miraculous healing, in **the name of Jesus**!

IN THE NAME OF JESUS, **during this ministry time in China,** many blind and diseased eye conditions were healed corporately, with one dynamic move of the Holy Spirit, without the laying on of hands. Bone conditions **were healed** and growths disappeared supernaturally. And there were many opportunities to receive the Salvation message in the process!

TODAY, I CHARGE YOU AND ASK YOU: <u>WILL YOU BE ONE OF GOD'S EARTHLY INHABITANTS/ VESSELS—USED FOR HIS KINGDOM PURPOSES</u>?

Insights: God's Use Of Earthly Inhabitants...

Can you imagine the Heavenly rewards which await you? Can you imagine the delightful, high praises and joy in Heaven even now, because of *the Eternal Fruit of souls as a result of your labor?*

Let us purpose in our hearts to BE—BE— the earthly vessels used for Kingdom Purposes in the place or station of your/our calling! May Heaven smile on your/our decisions, as we say: *YES, SEND ME IN JESUS NAME!*

WE MUST OCCUPY UNTIL HIS RETURN

The Work of the Servant-Prophet
Can Be Very Stressful
BUT, DON'T LOSE HEART!

At times, the battles have been intense and I have sustained battle scars. There have even been occasions when I called for paramedics and was taken to a hospital emergency room, fighting for my life! I THANK GOD for His Protective Covering, and the diligent Intercessory Prayer Warriors who petition the LORD in my behalf. (See Scriptures: Daniel 8:27...Acts 12:5)

On one such occasion, I was placed in the Emergency Room—awaiting testing—when one of God's Servants came into the room. She was either a Marketplace Servant serving as a nurse or an Angel, I was

> **TAKE COURAGE!**
>
> **THIS WORLD IS NOT OUR HOME!**
>
> We are the <u>Yet-to-Arrive</u> *Inhabitants* of Heaven!

Insights: God's Use Of Earthly Inhabitants...

not sure, as I never saw her again after she delivered her message to me, saying: "I am a Born Again Christian—a Catholic—but a Born Again Catholic. I know you are here under great stress, but you know that these things must come to pass so that our LORD can return." Then she added, with emphasis, "I will be praying for you."

The stress she was speaking of was the events—and victims—of the Burma Cyclone, the China Earthquake, and the Florida Fires—which had been set—and I had foreseen all of them. Now I had to witness that which I had seen by the Spirit, which spurred me to work even harder to complete and release my first Book, _TELL MY PEOPLE The Unalterable, Inconvenient Truths,_ with its urgent warnings to **get ready—be ready—for the End Time Foreclosure (His Rapture).** Nothing else will do!

In the meantime, I received the impact of fiery darts aimed to kill—which caught me by surprise as I was _interceding to intercept and defend_ an honored friend, another who walks the Front Lines for the Causes of Christ. This illness was strictly Spiritual Warfare, if I've ever witnessed any! And, I ended up standing in the gap, ultimately _replacing_ the one I was defending, complete with wires connecting me to a heart monitor, and blood pressure cuff, with the availability of oxygen and other emergency equipment which I had foreseen of the person I was defending.

In the *foreseen vision*—before the actual events—I was busy trying to find a phone to call for an ambulance, without success. Then, I was pulling out cords of different sizes and shapes, like the EKG and other equipment. The person I saw was in a desperate fight for life. But little did I know that I would be the one in this desperate struggle. For every *fore-vision*, there was a counterpart/parallel waiting <u>for me</u>.

But during my struggling encounters, the Lord provided more than 700 *rams-in-the-bush* through the prayers of Christian Muslims and other Christians <u>around the world</u> who were holding prayer sessions, <u>calling my name</u> before the Father!

I didn't know if I would make it! It was just that serious! Yet, as I am writing this book, I am THANKING GOD WITH ALL MY HEART for His Mercy, Grace, Protection and Restoration!

We must *think* and <u>persevere</u> like Daniel, who after THE EXPERIENCE and INTERPRETATION of HIS VISIONS of the evenings and mornings, stated:

"The visions of the evenings and mornings which was told is true; therefore, seal up the vision, for it refers to many days in the future.' <u>And I, Daniel,</u>

In these times
We have no choice
But to fight
The good fight
OF FAITH !

Insights: God's Use Of Earthly Inhabitants...

fainted and was sick for days; afterward I arose and went about the king's business. I was astonished by the vision; but no one understood." (Daniel 8:26-27)

No doubt there will be days of fatigue and sometimes of complete exhaustion, even as Daniel experienced, but be assured that rest will come and so will understanding, and renewal of strength for your journey! While we are not immune from attacks, we are certain of our ultimate VICTORY and SUCCESS through faith in Christ Jesus, who has won the victory on the Cross!

When the Lord said to me, **TAMPER with the traditions of man for ME**, I expected to experience success because:

SUCCESS is found in the doing of the **work** of the **One** Who called, **prepared** and sent you. Success will be rewarded when you DO that for which you are sent—not that which you elect to do.

HEAR THIS! HEAR THIS, says the Lord. **DO YOUR GOD GIVEN ASSIGNMENTS!**

Dear Reader: REFLECT NOW on the Will of the One Who sent you. Jesus was SENT to fulfill God's purpose in Him. He stayed focused on His PURPOSE—and so must we! He said, ***My food is to do the Will of Him Who SENT Me and to FINISH His work*** (John 4:34).

As the writing of this book comes to completion, the LORD is strongly directing my thoughts to the *heart* of His message for His People—the ones whose pulse is now racing with the desire to BE IN HIS SERVICE—to BE His **Third-Dimensional Servant.**

The Lord is saying: *You are my BUILDING BLOCKS to facilitate active Servant-hood in NEW DIMENSIONS of Service. There are many under-utilized Gifts and Talents. LOOSE THEM!*

The Office, duty and function of a Minister lies within the BODY OF CHRIST—THE CHURCH—whether clergy or not. All are instruments to be used for MY Causes! It is TIME for you to BE AGENTS of God IN SERVICE and ON DUTY!

With reflection on these words from the LORD, I am discovering more...

➤ National, Cultural and Societal *TRADITIONS* have built layer upon layer of barriers—thick walls—that keep people from knowing God, from intimate, personal relationship.

- In these End Times, the LORD is searching for Genuine—<u>Authentic</u>—Servants who will **challenge** the **traditional** customs, rituals, and folklore to DISCOVER GOD—WHO He is—and **discover** His Ways to live their lives. He searches for those who will step up—bring themselves and their neighbors back to HIM—His Heart/His Word/the Bible—His Ways.
- The LORD looks for AUTHENTIC Servant-hood—Servant-ministers who seek and follow HIS STANDARDS that He has set for this New Dimension of service—for this present End Time generation of Servants.
- Correction is needed in the "traditional" seminary-training of Servant/Ministers. God Himself is telling His Servants—through present-day Prophets—His RIGHT WAY. The Lord will *test* His people for authenticity—taking "stones" and polishing them into His Living "Gem Stones" FOR HIS OWN GOOD PLEASURES AND TREASURES!

The Apostle Luke records the following words, spoken by Jesus to His disciples:

"The harvest truly is great, but the laborers are few; therefore pray the Lord of the harvest to send out laborers into His harvest. (Luke 10:2)

**WHEN ALL IS SAID AND DONE
IT IS ALL ABOUT BEING *USED TO SERVE;*
BECOMING A YIELDED VESSEL ON THIS EARTH**

Insights: God's Use Of Earthly Inhabitants...

**FOR HIS KINGDOM PURPOSES
FOR THE CAUSES OF CHRIST!**

How will you respond?

**Are you willing to accept your *Role*,
Regardless of your Station or Position,
To BE the Lord's *Fishers-of-Men*
For the End Time Harvest of Souls?**

Selah
(Pause and Think on This)

***Selah*...THINK ON THIS!**

The LORD is saying to us today:

STAND STRONG!

OCCUPY UNTIL MY RETURN!

For Your Consideration

I believe there may be *curious readers* who have picked up this book, and have not yet accepted Jesus and His Gift of Salvation. There may also be those who now realize they need to re-establish their relationship with the LORD. So it is that I am placing this simple prayer here for your consideration. There is no "magic" in the specific words. It is your *heart's desire* that will become visible to the Lord. He awaits.

> Lord—God—here I am. You know me better than I know myself, and You've seen the sins of my life. I need You. I acknowledge the life, death and resurrection of Your Son, Jesus. My heart accepts Jesus as my Lord and Savior. From this moment and forever, please send Your Holy Spirit into my life to show me Your Ways. And, Lord, please give me the strength and wisdom to follow You into Eternity. Amen.

If you have prayed the prayer on the previous page and/or this book has impacted your life in any way, we would like to hear from you.

Please write to:

RIGHT WAY MINISTRIES INT'L., INC.
4311 Hampton Lane
Bowie, MD 20720
...or...
Email: **prophetessmaryj@vmdirect.com**

To schedule Prophetess Mary Johnson-Gordon for speaking engagements, please contact her @ the email address above.

Tax deductible donations to **Right Way Ministries**—in support of ministry travels, the production of additional books, and continuing outreach—may be made to the address above. *Right Way Ministries Int'l, Inc.* is a 501(c)(3), not-for-profit organization.

Additional copies of this book and Prophetess Mary's first book—**Tell My People the Unalterable Inconvenient Truths**—may be ordered directly from *Right Way Ministries* @ the above address, and from the publisher, Xulon Press.com/bookstore. Both books are also available on *Amazon* and *Barnes & Nobel.com,* and in most major bookstores; plus their **eBook** versions.

Acknowledgements

Throughout my life and ministry, many Ministers, Ministries, authors and individual people have followed the Lord's guidance and sown their gifts and talents into my endeavors. These precious people include Dr. Marilyn Hickey, Dr. Morris Cerullo, Reverend Dr. Lee P. Washington and numerous others.

I must also acknowledge the work of Paula A Price, Ph.D., who authored the book, *The Prophet's Dictionary: An Ultimate Guide to Supernatural Wisdom*. Having clear (and accurate) definitions of words and phrases which are often used in the prophetic was most valuable. I constantly thank God for her vital work and highly recommend that every reader consider adding a copy of this resource to their library.

ANNOUNCING

Future Books/Concepts
Now in the writing/editing Stages
By
Prophetess Mary L. Johnson-Gordon

INSIGHTS:
Scenes and Activities
***Witnessed* In Heaven**
With *Special Insights* Into God's Use
Of Heavenly Inhabitants
On Earth

INSIGHTS:
On the Other Side
Of TOMORROW—I SEE
A Message for Church Leaders and
Ministers

RIGHT WAY MINISTRIES INT'L, INC.
4311 Hampton Lane
Bowie, MD 20720
prophetessmaryj@vmdirect.com

GREAT REVIEWS

TELL MY PEOPLE
The Unalterable, Inconvenient Truths

For those who have been compelled to remain faithful to Christ's teachings in the midst of trials, this book not only offers explanations ...but also provides "from God" encouragement and purpose to your walk. R. Merrick

This book is Divinely Inspired! The compelling words of prophesy have burned a desire deep within me to step up to and maintain a higher standard in all that God has and is calling us to do. Truly Awesome from cover to cover!
Cleveland52

Autographed copies of this book
Available through:
Right Way Ministries Int'l., Inc.
4311 Hampton Lane
Bowie, MD 20720

Also available through *Xulon Press*/Bookstore; *Barnes & Nobel*.com, Amazon, most local bookstores and in the convenient eBook format.

ORDER FORM

Book(s):

    $15 each + $3.00 postage/handling

TELL MY PEOPLE...

Number of Copies:

INSIGHTS: God's Use of Earthly Inhabitants

Number of Copies:

[If requesting an *autographed* copy, please print the name(s) on the back of this section.]

[If book is to be mailed to an address other than the one below, please print on back of this section.]

Your Name:

Address:

City:

State: **Zip:**

Phone:

Email:

MAIL THIS FORM
And Check or Money Order TO:
Right Way Ministries Int'l, Inc.
4311 Hampton Lane
Bowie, MD 20720

Printed in the USA
CPSIA information can be obtained
at www.ICGtesting.com
LVHW041240051023
760079LV00002B/571